To my father, who taught me the joys of profanity; to my mother, who taught me the joys of pedagogy; and to you, dear reader, for letting me combine the two.

—*Juan Caballero*

To Carolina, Erin, and *El Club* for making Spanish fun. And to Beth and Miriam for being awesome; don't go to New York!
—*Nick Denton-Brown*

TABLE OF CONTENTS

Acknowledgments

Juan wishes he had the space and recollection to thank everyone who helped him with this book, but circumstances conspire against it. Chapters and entire draft copies were reviewed by María and Carlos Caballeros, Victor Goldgel Carballo, Gabrielle Wolodarski, and Ignacio Gatto Bellora. Roxana Fitch's website and the forum posters on wordreference.com also made this book possible, as did any number of anonymous wiki-ers, piroperos, smart-asses, graffiti artists, poets, and criminals. And thanks to Francine Masiello for recommending me for the job with her habitual overconfidence in my abilities.

Nick thanks Abby, Bryce, Juana, Lauren, and everybody else at Ulysses Press who listened to him bitch while this book got made. You guys rock.

USING THIS BOOK

This book was written with the assumption that you already know enough Spanish to get by. After all, this is a slang book, and slang tends to be the last thing you learn after getting down all the basic (and relatively useless) sayings, like "I live in the red house" and "Yes, I like the library very much, thank you." This is a book designed to take your Spanish to the next level. So if you're looking for a grammar lesson, you're in the wrong spot. But if you want to tell your friend that he has a tiny dick or to get rid of the douchebag hitting on you in the bar, this is the book for you.

Every phrase in *Dirty Spanish* is up-to-date slang. Except in special cases, the English is given first, followed by the Spanish. Sometimes the Spanish is given with alternatives (*gordo/a, tu/s*) to account for gender or plural differences. This isn't a grammar book and you're not an idiot, so we expect that you'll be able to figure it out without any more explanation.

Unlike other volumes in the *Dirty* series, this book covers not *one* language but many. That's because Spanish is *not* universal. Colombian slang is quite different from Spanish or Mexican slang. Most of the slang included here, though,

PRONOUNCING SPANISH)))

Speaking Spanish like a *pinche gringo* will make you seem like, well, a *pinche gringo,* and will raise the price of everything you want to buy in proportion to how annoying your accent is. It can even mark you as an easy target for pickpockets or muggers. So get your pronunciation straight. You have three golden rules to remember:

1. *Watch your damn vowels* already! Each vowel is essentially the same in every context:

> A is always like the "a" in "father."
>
> O is always like the "o" in "bone."
>
> I is always like the "ie" in "wiener."
>
> E is always like the "e" in "wet."
>
> U is always like the 'oo' in "poon," unless it comes after a "g" or a "q" and has no umlaut dots over it.

One of the biggest slipups that English speakers make when speaking Spanish is following the unconscious English pronunciation rules that make vowels change contextually, smuggling in foreign A's and turning every unstressed vowel into the "uuuuh" sound that Spanish speakers equate with the pronunciation of a village idiot (don't pruhtend you don't know whuht I'm talking uhbout).

2. *Pay attention to accents* when learning new words, and review the accent rules online or in your old grammar book before traveling. If you put the accent on the wrong syllable, people think you're saying another word, which, 99 percent of the time, is a word that doesn't exist. Americans are often shocked by not being understood for having fudged such a "minor" detail. But it's a major difference to Spanish speakers, so they, in turn, feel shocked when Americans walk around speaking gibberish and getting impatient with people.

3. *Don't over-pronounce.* Pay attention to local pronunciation and try to keep up; it makes you sound natural and cool. Vowels and syllables sometimes drop out of the middle of long words (*no te pr'ocupas*). D's between vowels at the end of words often drop out to make a vowel diphthong (it's *complicao*). Consonants at the end of words in an unstressed syllable, particularly D's and S's, often get underpronounced or forgotten altogether (*de vera', no te procupah*).

In the Caribbean, this process is taken one step further, frequently coming right in the middle of a word (*¡tu huele' como pe'cao!*). Also, syllable emphasis can change from city to city, overriding the normal accent-placement of a word. Subtle slipups like mixing up the pronunciation between S and Z or T and D, however the word might actually be spelled, can mark you as foreign. So listen closely to how people pronounce words you thought you already knew.

was chosen because it's easily understood in any Spanish-speaking country. But there are many terms that are region- or country-specific. For all of those, we've included abbreviations in parenthesis for the region or country where the phrase comes from:

COUNTRY	ABBREVIATION
Latin America	LatAm
South America	S.Am
Central America	CenAm
Southern Cone (Argentina, Chile, and Uruguay)	S.Cone
Caribbean	Carib
Andes	Andes
Mexico	Mex
Guatemala	Gua
El Salvador	ElS
Honduras	Hon
Nicaragua	Nic
Costa Rica	CoR
Panama	Pan
Cuba	Cub
Dominican Republic	DoR
Puerto Rico	PuR

COUNTRY	ABBREVIATION
Venezuela	Ven
Colombia	Col
Ecuador	Ecu
Peru	Per
Bolivia	Bol
Chile	Chi
Paraguay	Par
Uruguay	Uru
Argentina	Arg
Spain	Spn

Whenever a regional term is given in addition to a universal one, you can assume it'll sound more natural to someone from that region to hear that term. However, many regional terms are rapidly becoming international as Latin American media culture continues to globalize, and as teenagers all over the world listen to MP3s and download TV shows from around the Spanish-speaking globe.

If personal curiosity or professional demands require you to know exactly where a given term is used, or if you want to dive deeper into the seedy world of Spanish slang, the easiest place to start is online:

www.rae.es—The Real Académia Española's online dictionary may not always be cutting-edge for Latin American slang, but at least it's reliable and accurate.

www.jergasdehablahispana.org—Roxana Fitch's invaluable, free, and searchable dictionary houses a massive collection of slang, sorted by region.

forum.wordreference.com—The Word Reference forums are a thriving international community of professional translators and amateur linguists where you can get answers from real people in the field.

The best language teacher, however, will always be immersion. So get to traveling, do some downloading, start YouTube-ing, or, at the very least, go to the Hispanic part of town and strike up some conversations—just don't start with the "Angry Spanish" chapter!

Now take your *Dirty Spanish* and get down and dirty with it!

CHAPTER 1

HOWDY SPANISH
QUÉ TAL-'STELLANO

Spanish speakers in a friendly (or alcoholic) environment
rarely start conversations with an "*Hola*" or "*Buen día*." It's
more casual and common to head straight for a question,
even if it hangs in the air as hypothetical and unanswered
(some people routinely answer *¿Qué tal?* with…*¿Qué tal?*).

·····What's up?
¿Qué tal?

Many greetings, particularly short ones like *¿Qué dices?*,
sound best followed by an affectionate, mildly offensive
epithet (Tubby, Pizzaface, Nancy, Bigballs, whatever).

What's up?
¿Qué tal? | *¿Qué tal-co?* (S.Cone) | *¿Qué tal andas?* (Spn) |
¿Qué jais? (Mex)

What's happenin'?
¿Qué pasó?
Only tourists and people over 30 use *qué pasa* in the present tense
anymore.

What's goin' on?
¿Qué sapa?
Qué pasa in anagram form

What're you up to?
¿Qué haces?

What's the good word, Tubby?
*¿**Qué dices,** Gordo?*

Whatcha got?
¿A ver?

What the cock have you been up to?
¿A ver-ga?

What else is new with you?
De tu vida, ¿qué más?

What'd I miss?
¿Quihubo?

•••••How you doing?
¿Cómo andas?

As in English, once you're done with the initial niceties and greetings it's time to dig a little deeper and inquire about the person's life. Vague, fragmentary answers are the norm, so don't expect a lengthy response or even a complete sentence.

How you been doin'?
¿Cómo andas? | *¿Cómo andamio?* (S.Cone)

How's everything?
¿Cómo va todo?

> **Kickin' ass!**
> *¡De pelos!* | *¡A toda madre!* (Mex) | *¡De butaca!* (S.Cone)

> **Straight chillin'.**
> *Todo tránqui'.*

> **I'm all right.**
> *Ando ahí nomás.*

How 'bout things with you?
¿Y tus cosas?

> **Same as ever.**
> *Como siempre.*
>
> **Still putting around here, aren't I?**
> *Sigo por aquí, no? ; Aquí nomás.*

·····How's life, really?
¿Pero en serio, cómo te va la vida?

Even if your friend didn't mention any girl/boy/work/family troubles last time you talked, it's fair game to ask them about it point-blank if you've heard things on the grapevine.

> **What's the dilly with…?**
> *¿Qué onda con…?*
>
> **What's the latest with…?**
> *¿Qué cuentas sobre…? ; ¿Qué se cuenta de…?*
>
>> **your old lady?**
>> *la vieja?*
>>
>> **the ball-n-chain?**
>> *la jefa? ; la domadora?*
>>
>> **your folks?**
>> *los viejos? | los tatas? (Mex)*
>
> The whole situation is **seriously fucked**.
> *Todo el asunto está **seriamente jodido**.*
>
> **I don't even wanna talk about it.**
> *Ni hablar.*
>
> What's happenin' with that **little venture**?
> *¿Que pasó con ese **bisnes**?*
>
>> It's **scraping by**.
>> ***En algo** está.*
>
> How's your **chump job**?
> *¿Qué pasó con el **curro**? (Spn) | …la **chamba**? (Mex) | …la **changa**? (S.Cone) | …el **camello**? (Andes)*

Gettin' paid, at least.
Me pagan, por lo menos.

They're really **wiping their asses** with me.
*Me están **pasando por el culo**.*

·····Look who showed up!
¡Mira quien apareció!

It's common among good friends to express exaggerated surprise or joy at an arrival, particularly a late one. These expressions seem dramatic in English, but are a normal part of interacting in Spanish-speaking lands. It's common in these situations to call someone by a nickname that would, in other contexts, be way more offensive, like *Pendejo de mierda* (Total fucker) or *Hijo de la gran puta* (Son of a royal whore).

Look who **showed up!**
*¡Mira quien **apareció**! ; ¡...**volvió**!*

You made it, Dopey!
*¡**Caíste**, salame!* (S.Cone)

They let you out!
¡Te dejaron salir!

Here he is, **back from the dead!**
*¡Uppaa, **llegó el desaparecido**!*
Be careful with this one in the Southern Cone, where *"los desaparecidos"* refers to people who "disappeared" during various murder-happy dictatorships.

Just when we were too few, and then...
¡Tras que éramos pocos, y...

Granny gave birth!
parió la abuela!
Don't ask me why this perverse spectacle would make for a kick-ass party...but it is definitely a common saying!

my brother hired a **drag queen!**
*mi hermano trajo un **travestí**!*

the wild beast / the deaf girl / so-and-so showed up!
llegó la bestia / la sorda / fulano!

Doofus showed up!
cayó el tronco!

·····Hey!
¡Oye!

At some point, you'll probably need to catch someone's attention in a crowded street, open-air market, barfight, or orgy. There are a bunch of ways to do so, but most are pretty regional—there's no universal "hey" aside from "*oye*" (listen) and "*mira*" (look), and even those have regional connotations (like in Argentina, where they sound more confrontational, like "listen up!").

Hey!
¡Oye! | ¡Aguas! (Mex) *| ¡Mare!* (Mex) *| ¡Ala!* (Andes) *| ¡Che!* (S.Cone)
Che is a trademark of the Argentine dialect, where it means both "hey" and "guy." Borges once "Argentinized" the story of Caesar and Brutus by substituting the famous "*et tu, Brute*?" with an angry "*¡Pero, che!*"

Hey, now!
¡Épale!

Watch out! / Eeeasy there.
¡Eeeeeeh-pa!

Look!
¡Mira!

Listen.
¡Oye!

Listen up, deaf guy!
¡Oye, sordo! | ¡Oye, teniente! (Spn)

Wake up, space-cadet!
¡Oye, ausente! ; ¡Oye, zombi!

Check this out!
¡Chéquele!

Check out that hairy guy's **back-bush!**
¡Chéque la barba dorsal que tiene ese gorila!

·····Goodbye
Adiós

For some reason, Spanish farewells are a blank check for oorniness. *Ciao*, the most common slang for "good-bye," is sometimes spelled phonetically, so don't be battled by a "chau" or a "chao" on a billboard or in a comic book. *Ciao* is so common that many Latin Americans would be surprised if you told them it's actually Italian.

Later!
¡Ciao!

Lates!
¡Chabela! ; ¡Chavela!
From "*Ciao, bella*"

In a while, crocodile.
Chaufa. (Per)
This is a horrible Peruvian pun on Chinese food: "ciaofun."

Bye y'all. (hick, countryish way of saying "bye")
Chado. (Andes)

See ya around!
¡Ahí nos vemos!

See ya in a bit!
¡Ahí nos vidrios!

Toodles!
¡Ahí nos Belmont! (Chi)

We're outta here.
Nosotros nos huimos.

See ya **later**.
¡Hasta luego!

L8R.
Elejota.
The phonetic pronunciation of *L.J.*, which is the abbreviation for *los juimos*, Chilean slang for "Let's go."

Until next time!
¡Hasta la próxima!

Smell ya later!
¡Hasta el cante! (Spn) | *¡Hasta el hornazo!* (Mex) | *¡Hasta la chucha!* (Andes) | *¡Hasta la baranda!* (S.Cone)

·····Blessings and graces
Bendiciones y gracias

Catholicism is as widespread in Spain and Latin America as advertising is in America or drinking is in Ireland. And just as the British will say "Cheers" as you hand them an Alcoholics Anonymous pamphlet, many Spanish speakers will literally bless you even if you're wearing a yarmulke and a giant star of David.

May God go with you.
Que vaya Dios contigo.

Fare thee well.
Que le vaya bien.

May God watch over you.
Que Dios te guarde.

May things go swell for you.
Que te vaya bonito.

If God so wills, no more freeways will collapse.
Si Dios quiere, no se derrumbarán más autopistas.

God and the new budget willing, we'll get a raise on the 4th.
Mediante Dios y el presupuesto nuevo, nos dan un aumento de sueldo el día 4.

I pray to God that my car won't fail me again.
Ojalá que no me falle el coche de nuevo.

·····Sorry
Sori

In Spanish, you don't so much apologize as plead distraction, momentary lapse of reason, ill luck, or simply general incompetence. Most Spanish speakers use self-deprecation to extract themselves from a sticky situation rather than beg forgiveness. So if you get caught cheating on your girlfriend or boyfriend, just say, "Whoops, aren't I the sillyhead!" and then grin until your cheeks hurt.

Sorry!
¡Perdón! ; ¡Sorri! ; ¡Sori!

I'm really, really sorry!
¡Lo siento muchísimo!

My bad.
Emece.
As in "M.C.": mea culpa

My deepest **apologies**
*¡Mil **disculpas**!*

I crossed the line.
Me pasé de la raya.

Forgive me.
Perdóname.

I'm so embarrassed!
¡Qué vergüenza! | *¡Qué corte!* (Spn)

I'm so humiliated!
¡Qué pena me da!

What a stupid thing to do!
¡Qué idiotez! ; ¡Qué huevada!

What a fuck-up!
¡Qué cagazón! (Mex) | *¡Qué boludez!* (S.Cone)

·····Get over it
Aguántatelo

If apologizing doesn't get you off the hook, you should move for a full dismissal of charges. Some people just won't listen to reason and need to be told to shut the hell up and stop acting like a little bitch.

> **Let's not get carried away.**
> *No es para tanto.*

> **It's not what it looks like!**
> *¡No es lo que parece!*

> **I didn't mean to.**
> *Fue sin querer.*

> I didn't mean to shit in your **bidet**!
> *¡Cagué en tu **bidet** sin querer!*

> Oh, don't **make a scene**!
> *¡Ay, no **armes un escándolo**!*

> **Take it easy.**
> *Tómalo con calma.*

> Chill out, man, it's **just a dribble** of urine.
> *Calma, hombre, es **un chorrito** de orina **nomás**.*

·····'Scuse me
'Miso

Latins don't have many ways of saying "excuse me." As the old saying goes, *Mejor pedir perdón que pedir permiso* (Better to apologize later than ask permission beforehand).

> **Excuse me.**
> *Con permiso.*

> **'Scuse me.**
> *Permiso.*

Meepmeep.
'Miso-miso.

Make way, I'm in a rush.
***Abre paso**, vengo apurado.*

Watch out!
¡Cuidado!

Back in a flash!
¡Vuelvo rapidingo!

·····Please
Porfa

Spanish slang is supertheatrical—you'll often see adults pleading like children for a simple favor. That's because you don't merely ask someone for something; you paint them as your supreme benefactor, a noble gaucho and angelic do-gooder who would forever be immortalized in song if they could somehow bring it upon themselves to pass the damn salt.

Pleeeeease!
¡Poorfaa!

Pretty please!
¡Plis-plis!

HELP A BROTHER OUT»

ÉCHAME UN CABLE, 'MANO

Be a pal.	*Sé buen amigo.*
Be a buddy.	*Sé valedor.* [Mex]
Be a team-player.	*Sé jalador.* [Mex]
Be a stand-up dude.	*Sé paleta.* [Chi]
Be a real chum.	*Sé tronco.*

Please do me **the favor**.
*Por favor, hágame **el favor**.* | *...**la gauchada*** (S.Cone) | *...**la volada*** (CenAm) | *...**el cruce*** (Col)

You scratch my back and I'll scratch yours.
¡Hazme un cambalache!

Please **have the decency** to shut that gossiping mouth of yours.
***Tenga la bondad** de callar esa boca chismosa, por favor.*

·····Good to meet ya
Un placer darte a conocer

After meeting someone, it's always nice to express your pleasure at having done so. People like to be liked. Go figure.

Pleased to meet you.
Mucho gusto.

Please-ta meetcha.
'Chogusto.

¡NTRODUCiNG YOURSƎLF)))

My name is Ingelbert.
Me llamo Ingelberto.

I'm from Germany.
Vengo de Alemania.

I'm six-foot-four and hung like a donkey.
Mido dos metros y traigo un bulto como un burro.

They call me the Princess.
Me llaman la Princesa.

I'm Canadian. It's like an American, except without a gun.
Soy canadiense. Es como un yanqui, pero sin arma.

But I can still snap you like a twig, so stay where you are.
Igual puedo romperte como una paja, entonces quédate ahí.

I'm charmed.
Encantado.

The pleasure is all mine.
El placer es todo mío.

Have a good one.
Que le vaya bien.

Hopefully, we'll **bump into each other** again.
*A ver si **nos encontramos** por ahí.*

·····What do you do for fun?
¿Cómo te diviertes?

Once you've established that someone's gonna be at your table for a while and you've exhausted all the small talk, it's far more acceptable than in the U.S. to press for personal details.

Where are your people from?
*¿De donde viene **tu gente**?*

How long have you lived in the city?
¿Desde cuándo has vivido en la ciudad?

Where were you raised?
¿Dónde te criaste?

How single are you, exactly?
*¿**Cuán soltero** estás, de hecho?*

Where'd you learn **to open bottles** like that?
*¿Dónde aprendiste **a descorchar botellas** así?*

Would you give me **a private lesson**?
*¿Me darías **una lección privada**?*

What team do you play for, if you don't mind my asking?
*¿**Para qué equipo juegas**, si no te molesta la pregunta?*

DOUBLE MEANINGS)))

DOBLE-SENTIDOS

After you've been speaking Spanish for a while, you'll start to notice how a lot of it can be taken as innocent dialogue or as sexually charged innuendo.

Please-ta meetcha, what *was* it again?
Chogusto, ¿cómo era?

It's Paco, and the **deep pleasure** has been all mine, **Linda (Beautiful)**.
*Es Paco, y el **placer hondo** ha sido todo mío, Linda.*

But my name is Anna.
Pero yo me llamo Anna.

As I well know already.
Ya lo sé a fondo.

Are you **pulling my leg**?
*¿Me estás **cachondeando**?*
Cachondeando is a versatile word that refers to bullshitting, flirting, and when a dog humps your leg.

Nothing of the sort, my lady; on the contrary, I am entirely **at your disposal**.
Nada de eso, mi reina; yo estoy, todo lo contrario, entéramente a tus órdenes.

Well, if you are "entirely," maybe I'll have some **gruntwork** for you one of these days.
*Bueno, si lo eres "enteramente," acaso tendré alguna **faena** para vos un día de estos.*

CHAPTER 2

FRIENDLY SPANISH
QUÉ TAL-'STELLANO

The best way to internalize the rhythms of Spanish-speaking society is to watch *telenovelas* for a few hours a day and read some smutty comics. These pulpy media are a great way to sharpen your verbal and judgmental skills on fictional victims.

•••••Real friends
Amigotes

Spanish-speakers have tons of words to describe their range of friends, many based on degrees of closeness. Even more so than usual, these terms vary not only from country to country, but also within countries, between classes, between cities, or even by neighborhood or social circle.

Best-bud
Amigote/a | cuate/a (CenAm)

> He's my **best friend** from back in the day.
> *Es mi **amigote** desde hace mucho.*

Old school chum
El/La cole (short for *colega*)

> I miss my **old school friends**.
> *Estraño a mis **coles**.*

A girl (young)
Una nena

> Who's that **little girl**?
> *Esa **nena**, ¿quién es?*

Some random dude
Un tipo cualquiera | *Un tío cualquiera* (Spn)

> She hooked up with **some random dude** last night.
> *Ella se enrolló con **un tipo cualquiera** anoche.*

Punk kid
Chamaco/a (Mex) | *Pibe/a* (S.Cone) | *Chaval/a* (Sp)

> Don't get huffy, he's just a **punk kid**.
> *No te encabrones, es un **chamaco** nomás.*

A chick
Una chava | *Una mina* (S.Cone)

> Your sister's a **cool chick**.
> *Tu hermana es **buena chava**.*

A bastard
Un cabrón/ona (Mex)

> Your brother's a **real bastard**.
> *Tu hermano es **un cabronazo**.*

My bro
Mi 'mano | *Mi carnal* (Mex)

> How you been, **bro**?
> *¿Cómo viene la cosa, **'mano**?*

My sis
Mi 'mana

> What's new, **sis**?
> *¿Qué hay de nuevo, **'mana**?*

My boy
Mi compa'

> We've been **boys** forever.
> *Somos **compas** desde siempre.*

My girl
Mi comay

> Don't worry about her; she's **my girl**.
> *No te preocupes por ella—es **mi comay**.*

The guys
Los muchachos

> He's fooling around with **the guys**.
> *El está al pedo con **los muchachos**.*

Bosom buddies
Amigos del alma

> They've been **bosom buddies** since they were little.
> *Han sido **amigos del alma** desde chicos.*

My confidant
Mi tumba
This derives from the old saying "Take it to your tomb."

> I only tell you this 'cuz you're **my confidant**,
> understand?
> *Contártelo a ti es contárselo a **mi tumba**, ¿entiendes?*

Good people
Buena gente

> You can trust Jaime, he's **good people**.
> *Puedes confiar en Jaime, es **buena gente**.*

·····Duuuuuuude
Chavóoooon

As in any language, there are some names you say and others you just yell drunkenly across the bar at the end of the night. Here are the more affectionate ways to holler at your dude-bros.

Man!
¡Macho!

Dude!
¡Chavo!

WHEN IN ROME...DON'T CALL THEM ROMANS)))

Know how people in New York like to call themselves New Yorkers and say they live in the Big Apple? Well, they stole that habit from Spanish speakers just like they stole Manhattan from the Indians. Here's a handy chart of the affectionate names Spanish speakers call themselves and their cities.

People who live in:	Call themselves:	And their city:
Buenos Aires	Porteños	Baires, Buesas
Madrid	Madrileños, Gatos	El Foro
Barcelona	Barceloneses, Barcelona	Barna, Barça
Mexico City	Chilangos	El Monstruo
Guadalajara	Tapatios	Guanatas
Lima	Limeños, Zapallos	
Guatemala City	Chapines	
El Salvador	Guanacos	
Nicaragua	Nicas	
Costa Rica	Ticos	

Duuuuuuude!
¡Chavóoooon!

Chicky!
¡Chava!

Sweetheart!
¡Queriiido! (Arg)
This literally means "beloved," but somehow, even the manliest working-class Argies call each other this with no homoerotic connotation whatsoever.

·····Moms and pops
Mami y tata

Everyone's got a mother and a father. Unless you are an orphan, were born to gay parents, or were painfully abandoned as a child—in which case you can pretend your therapist is your *madre de leche*.

Daddy
Papi | *Pai* (Carib) | *Papay* (Andes)
In the mouth of an adult, *papi* usually has the same nasty connotation that "daddy" would have in English, as in "Oooh, Daddy, don't stop!"

Dad
Papá | *Apá* (Mex)

Pops
El tata (LatAm) | *El taita* (Carib, Andes)

My old man/My old lady
Mi viejo/Mi vieja

A bad father
El pudre
This pun on *padre* literally means, "he rots."

Doofus dad
El tato
Tato literally connotes a stutterer with a hard-T speech impediment.

Mommy
Mamá | *Amá* (Mex) | *Mamay* (Andes)

Moms
Mami | Mai (Carib)

Stepmother (wicked or otherwise)
La madrastra
The suffix "-*astra*" means "secondary" (and implies "wicked") in many other family-terms: *padrastro, abuelastra, hermanastro*…

Mother figure / adoptive mother
Madre de leche

You got momma's-boy-itis.
Tienes la mamitis.

Your mom!
¡La madre que te parió!

You talkin' about my mom?
¿Estás mentando a mi madre?

·····Other fam
Otros en la fami

Most nicknames for family members are pretty regional, but here are the universal basics.

Get out the rocker for **Gramps**.
*Traiga la mecedora para **el abue'**. | ...**el yayo*** (Spn) | ...**el nono*** (S.Cone, from the Italian)

Your **gramma** is still kinda hot.
*Tu **abue'** sigue medio buena. | ...**yaya**...* (Spn) | *...**nona**...* (S.Cone)

Easy there, **old-timer**.
*Con calma, **anciano/a**. | ...**ruco/a*** (Mex)

You better marry him quick if don't want an **illegitimate son**.
*Tienes que casarte pronto si no quieres un **hijo natural**.*

The title of my honors thesis is **Fatherless Sons**: The Legacy of Colonialism.
*El título de mi tesis de honores es **Hijos espurios**: legados del colonialismo.*

Fidel Castro was the **bastard son** of a sugar planter.
*Fidel Castro fue el **hijo bastardo** de un hacendado de azúcar.* | *...**guacho**... (S.Cone)*

He think he's the **head of the household**, but his wife brings home the bacon.
*El se piensa **padre de familia**, pero la esposa trae la lana.*

Man, your wife plays the **housewife**, but she couldn't bake you a *tres leches* to save her life.
*Ufa, tu mujer se viste bien de **madre de familia**, pero ni soñar de que te haga un tres leches como la gente.*

That boy's one **apple that didn't fall far from the tree**.
*Eso chico **sí que salió hijo de su padre/madre**.*

·····Booty calls
Consuelos sexuales

Most Spanish-speakers don't think of sexual adventures as immoral or depraved unless they're jealous old schoolmarms addicted to *telenovelas*. And even then there's something tongue-in-cheek about their aspersions. These handy names for all the shades of gray between singledom and married life are less judgmental than their English equivalents. Don't be shocked to hear them used between people who don't know each other very well.

I gotta find me a...
Necesito encontrarme un/una...

    boyfriend/ girlfriend
    novio/novia

    live-in girlfriend
    arrejuntada |
    juntada (CenAm)

lover
amante
Amante doesn't always imply sex, just intensity—so don't panic if someone says your 10-year-old sister has a lover!

companion / partner (domestic)
'ñera/'ñero

friend with benefits
amigovio/a
amigo + novio = amigovio

fuckbuddy
tragon/a
This awesome word literally means "expert swallower" or "gulper." With a name like that, who *wouldn't* want a fuckbuddy?

booty call
consuelo sexual

Sounds like you need **to make a booty call**.
*Suena como que necesitas **hacerte una llamada caliente**.*

little somethin' on the side
segundo frente

It's too early for that, we're still in **second gear**.
*Es temprano para eso, todavía estamos en **grado dos**.*

LOVEY-DOVEY NICKNAMES)))

AMORÍFICOS

My better half	*Mi media naranja*
My sweetheart	*Mi corazón*
The apple of my eye	*Alma de mi vida*
My old man	*Mi mareado* [Mex]
My sweetness	*Mi cariño*
My old lady	*Mi negra** [Arg]

* This term has, in most contexts, lost any [conscious] racial meaning it historically had.

You guys aren't even **shacking up** yet?
*¿Ustedes nisiquiera **se han arrejuntado**?*

•••••Office dynamics
Dinámica de oficina

Real life is just like *The Office*, except sad and not funny. Like most people, you probably hate your job because you're surrounded by incompetent assholes, brown-nosing suckups, and shitty coworkers with almost as many annoying personal habits as the number of hours of your life you've wasted in their company. Here are some ways for you to defame all those no-talent ass-clowns behind their backs.

I share my cubicle with a real **suckup**.
*Comparto mi cubículo con un **lambiscón/a** total.*

What an **ass-kisser**!
*¡Qué **lameculos**! | ¡Qué **chupaculos**!* (S.Cone)

You gotta be a **yes-man** to get ahead.
*Tienes que ser un **pelotillero/a** para sobresalir.*

That **goody two-shoes** never calls in sick.
*Ese **beato/a** nunca se reporta enfermo/a.*

Just don't let **Mr. Overtime** get involved. (no talent, buckets of extra effort)
*No dejes que se meta **el Empollón**.*
In school or research-oriented professions like law, you can also use the more vivid *tragalibros*.

Watch out, here comes the **whipcracker**.
*Ojo, que viene el **tirante**. | ...el **bretel*** (S.Cone)

Don't leave the decision up to that **waffler**.
*No dejes la decisión al **panqueque** ese.*

An opportunist like her is always waiting to **stab you in the back**.
*Una **veleta** como ella siempre está dispuesta a darte **la puñalada trapera**.*
Una veleta means "weathervane," as in: faces wherever the wind's blowing.

I gotta pull the deadweight of my **slacker** coworkers.
*Estoy condenado al remo por los **desganados** de mis colegas.*

I'm a **do-nothing** and I do it well.
*Soy un **quedado** y me quedo muy bien.* | *...un **queso**...* (S.Cone)

He would be a janitor if he **weren't the boss's nephew**.
*Sería el conserje si **no tuviera el padre alcalde**.*

You sure love **to brown-nose** him, don'tcha?
*¿Gozas mucho de **chuparle las medias**, o no?* | *...**hacerle la pelota**...* (Spn)

•••••Life of the party
El vacilón

Every great party I've ever been to has had some awesome guy in a bizarro costume jumping on the couch and spraying Jaeger across the room like he just won the World Series. Unfortunately, I've been to as many lame-ass parties populated by moochers, buzzkills, and straight-up nerds, the type of puritanical nancies who suddenly get too tired to play any more strip poker on the same hand they lose their pants. So quit acting like a *pinchaglobos*, grab the Don Julio, and *quítate los pantalones* already!

You are a/the...
¡Eres un/una...!

He/She is (a)...
¡El/Ella es (un/una)...!

What a...
¡Qué...!

Quit being so/such a...
¡No seas tan/un/una...!

> **life of the party**
> *vacilón/ona*

party animal
calavera

party pooper
aguafiestas

buzzkill
cortamambos

wet blanket
pinchaglobos

freeloader
aprovechado | *piola* (S.Cone)

moocher
remo
A *remo* is an oar—something that never pulls its own weight!

professional crasher
paracaidista

social butterfly / quick friend
amiguero/a (LatAm) | *macanudo/a* (S.Cone)
Outside the Southern Cone, *macanudo* just means
"upstanding" or "morally good."

out of it, in one's own world
ensimismado/a

phoney
plástico/a

sheltered nerd
nerdo | *zanahoria* (Andes) | *zapallo* (S.Cone)

boring / wearisome
pesado/a | *pelma* (Spn)

conversational zero
lastre ("deadweight") | *plomazo/a* ("a big lead weight")

Valium on legs
soporífico/a ("a sedative")

show-off
fanfarrón/ona

real talker
picudo/a (Mex)

·····Class
Cuna

Americans are sometimes shocked at how openly people in other countries talk about class. And class-talk is super common in Latin America and Spain, where there existed an honored aristocracy until quite recently (in many areas, the last names of the moneyed class still haven't changed). So don't be surprised when casual conversation takes a sudden turn for the socioeconomic.

He/She is so...
El/Ella es tan...

uppity
afectado/a

pretentious
agrandado/a | pituco/a (S.Cone, Andes)

TAKING THEM DOWN A NOTCH)))

BAJÁNDOLES LOS HUMOS

Stuck up	*Fufurufo/a*
Ned Flanders	*Santurrón/Santurrona*
Gullible	*Ñoño/a*
Lowlife	*Canalla*
Laughingstock	*Un/una hazmerreír*
Ex-con (lit. or fig.)	*Reo/a*
Crass	*Grosero/a*
Brat	*Un/una niñato/a*
Bossy	*Mandón/Mandona*
A curmudgeon	*Un/una infeliz*
Pussy-whipped	*Un "siquerida"* (a "Yes, dear!")
Hermit	*Padre del yermo*
A decrepit old geezer	*Un vejestorio decrépito*

fake
plástico/a

common
ordinario/a

tacky
cursi

trashy
jarca

chi-chi
paquete

blue-blooded
de alcurnia | *de cuna* (S.Cone)

working-class
de plebea

top-notch
de categoría | *de catego* (Mex)

How did that **hoochie** manage to marry a doctor?
*¿Cómo llegó a casarse con un doctor esa **guarra**?*

She wishes she was an **A-list celebrity**.
*Ella sueña con ser una **de la farándula**.*

All those fashion designers in Mexico city are just
wannabe Euros.
*Todos esos diseñadores de moda chilangos son **unos
europizantes**. | ...**unos malinchistas** (Mex)*
Everyone in Mexico considers Mexico City to be full of Eurocentric,
wannabe sellouts—kinda like how Texans think of L.A.

I like **girls from good homes**.
*Por mi parte, yo prefiero a **las niñas bien**.*

·····The gays
Los gay

Despite the "macho" reputation, the Hispanic world has
plenty of queers, and gay tourism is booming (with tons of
bearded dudes, beaches galore, and never-ending parades
of slushy drinks sipped out of fruit husks, it's just like San

Francisco but warmer). Spanish speakers neutralize gay-bashing terms by using them affectionately, calling one another "Faggy" (*Marica*), for instance, just as they call each other "Fatty" (*Gordito*). But the interpretation is all in your tone, so make sure you use the following words like a sweetly cooing trannybar hostess and not some degenerate skinhead.

Since when does he/she dress like a…?
¿Desde cuando se viste el/ella como…?

faggot
un maricón | un joto (Mex)

fag / faggy
un marica
If you hear *marica* bandied about in Colombia, don't freak out. Colombians use this word liberally to mean "buddy" or "pal."

nancy
una mariposa
Literally, "a butterfly"

queen
un mariposo ; una reina

twink
una mariquita

femme
un hembra

butch
una macho | una machona (Andes, S.Cone) | *una machorra* (Mex)

bulldyke
una marimacha

lesbo
una tortillera (Mex) | *una arepera* (Andes)

drag queen
un travestí ; una reina

Did you see him **fagging out** at the party last night?
*¿Lo viste **volteándose** anoche en la fiesta?*

He's totally **bent**.
*Es un **volteado** total.*

I bet she **plays for both teams**.
*Ella debe **jugar en las dos direcciones**.*

Manuel's **wifey** is a banker named Ezekiel.
*El **hembrito** de Manuel es un banquero que se llama Ezequiel.*

CHAPTER 3

PARTY SPANISH
CASTELLANO FIESTERO

Spanish speakers will party for any reason and without warning. These little lessons will show how to pick your path through *partilandia* without dumping on anyone's vibe, which is to say, *sin echar agua en la fiesta de nadie*.

·····Where the party at?
¿Dónde hay pachanga?

The word *fiesta* is a general term that includes the craziest bachelor party of your life, as well as your kid sister's 12th birthday party (not to be confused with her 15th, which you might actually want to go to). Know what you're being invited to before you give a yea or a nay.

We should hit up that...
Debemos meternos en ese/esa...

Wanna crash a...?
¿Quieres colarte en un/una...?

    house party
    pachanga (Mex) | *jarana* (Spn)

block party
festividad de barrio

dance club
disco club (Spn) | *boliche* (S.Cone, Andes)

dive bar
antro barato (Mex)

fun little shindig between friends
party ; pari

little party in someone's apartment
fiestita depto

BBQ
asado (CenAm) | *barbacoa* (Carib)

Ranch party
fiesta ranchera; fiesta de quinta (more upscale)
These are massive ragers where everyone crashes in a huge ranch house—no neighbors, no cops—for a few days!

high-roller party
fiesta paquete

Golden Wedding Anniversary Celebration
Festejo del aniversario de oro

masquerade
baile de máscaras
These are still common, though mostly just in bordellos these days.

A TOTAL FREE-FOR-ALL》》

UN LÍN TOTAL

Here are some terms for those parties that require serious mopping-up or deep-carpet cleaning, if not ball-posting, afterward.

A huge blow-out	*Un reventón*
A real riot	*Un bochinche*
Utter chaos	*Un barullo*
A first-rate megaparty	*Un festejón de primera*
A rager	*Un bacanal*
No holds barred	*Deschavetado* [LatAm]

·····Having fun?
¿Divertiéndote?

An important part of taking someone out is checking in and taking measurements on the fun-o-meter. Here's some vocab useful for that kind of shiz.

You **having fun**?
*¿Estás **disfrutando**?*

> **Yeah, this place doesn't suck.**
> *Wow, genial, este lugar.*
> *Wow*, pronounced flatly enough, is clearly sarcastic even through the worst accent.
>
> **This little place is bumpin'!**
> *¡Este rinconcito está **a toda madre**!* (Mex)
>
> **I feel like cutting loose.**
> *Me da por **vacilar**.*
>
> **Check out all the hotties!**
> *¡Mírale las **bomboncitas**!*

Let's go...
¡Vámonos a...!

> **hit on some girls/some guys**
> *ligarnos unas chicas/unos tíos*

get a drink
echar un trago

get our groove on
soltar una juerga

get crunk
deschavetarnos (LatAm)

I'm **really digging** what the DJ is spinning.
*Estoy **gozando** mucho lo que está tocando el DJ.*

Check it out, your friend's really **getting down**!
*¡Éjele, que tu amigo está **vacilando**!*

Yeah, she's **grinding all over** that guy.
*Sí, ella le está **haciendo un buen perreo**.*

This place is seriously **a dive**!
*En serio que este lugar es **un tugurio**.*
Literally, "a shepherd's hut"

Yeah man, **it blows**.
*Simón, **es una mierda**.*

Let's get out of this **shithole**.
*Larguémonos de este **pedorreo**.*

•••••Cheers
Salud

As part of Europe, Spain has a culture of hard drinking similar to our Anglo-American one. Social interactions are often well-lubricated, complete with drinking songs and games. In Latin America, however, binge drinking is seen as more pathetic or self-destructive than social or funny, and having one too many isn't usually something to brag about the way it is in American frat culture.

Let's go for **a drink**.
*Vamonos por **un trago**.* | *...**un chupo*** (S.Cone)

Wanna **knock back a few**?
*¿Quieres **echar unas copas**?* | *...**unos copetes*** (Chi)

Cheers! A toast!
¡Salud! ¡Brindis!

To good friends!
¡Brindemos por los amigotes!

To Pancho Villa, and his rebel 'stache!
¡A Pancho Villa, y su bigote bandido!

Bottoms up!
¡Arriba, abajo, al centro, y adentro!
Say the words to this toast as you move your glass high
(*arriba*), low (*abajo*), toward the center (*al centro*), and then
into your mouth in one quick drag.

Gimme a…
Dame…

>**beer**
>*una cerveza*
>
>**brewskie**
>*una chela* (LatAm) | *una birra* (S.Cone, Andes) |
>*una cheve* (Mex)
>
>**cheap beer**
>*una cerveza barata*
>
>**third-rate beer**
>*una cerveza de tercera*

beer on tap
una cerveza tirada

bottle of beer
una botella de cerveza

a shot
un trago carto | un traguito chupito (Spn) |
caballito (Mex)

Let's pound these shots.
Trágemonos estos traguitos.

Hey, bartender, **a round** for my friends.
*Oye, camarero, **una ronda** para mis amigos.*

Chug! Chug! Chug!
¡Traga! ¡Traga! ¡Traga!

·····Hard liquor
Aguardientes

With so many gloriously fermentable ingredients at their disposal, Spanish speakers have a plethora of specialty drinks that they can do like no others.

Barkeep, set me up with a splash of…
Mozo, alcánzame un chorro de…

Tequila
Made from the blue agave or *maguey* cactus, Tequila has been central to Mexican drunkenness since pre-Columbian times, when drinking *pulque* (an undistilled form you can still get in some rural areas) was a sacred and often hallucinogenic way of worshipping *Mayáhuel*, the goddess of rowdiness, fertility, and peeing yourself in public.

Mezcal
Jalisco may have a trademark on *tequila*, but old-school Oaxaca's got its own variation: the *pulque*-like and earthy *mezcal* in which swims the larva of the famous *hypopta agavis* worm. Yum!

Daquirí
OK, maybe you think it's tacky because it's been your mom's favorite drink since that *Princess* cruise to Orlando. But hey, in climates where fresh, ripe fruit is dirt-cheap and available year-round, it belongs in your cocktail.

¡Cuba Libre!
Somehow squeezing half a lime into a rum-n-coke is a quantum leap forward. It also gives you a cool slogan to shout in public. But be careful, the name comes from the revolution *before* The Revolution, so you might wanna call it a *ron con coca y lima* if you're actually in Cuba ordering this with Communist Party members around.

Telegrama
If you like mint but think mojitos and juleps are too sweet, maybe you'll like this rum and crème de menthe on ice.

Calambuco
A Cuban moonshine rum—though you might not wanna get too adventurous with drinks that could *blind* you.

Chicha
This is a general category of Andean corn-based drinks, usually but not always fermented and alcoholic. In Peru, old women sometimes start the fermentation process by chewing on the corn and spitting it out. Mmmmmm, nothing beats old lady spit!

Pisco Sour
Peru's famous distilled brandy *pisco* is mysteriously mellowed out when you add it to whipped raw egg whites, simple syrup, a dash of bitters, and the juice of a very acidic Peruvian lime.

Sangría
Many of Spain's full-bodied wines are fierce and vinegary. That's why adding sweet fruit like apples and a tart middleman like blood orange juice isn't just a good idea, it's a goddamn national treasure.

·····Drunkenness
Borrachera

Try extra hard to memorize these phrases. By the time you actually need them, there's no way in hell you'll be able to pull out this book and look 'em up.

I am...
Estoy...

American girls love to get...
A las chicas norteamericanas les encanta ponerse...

> **drunk**
> *borracho/a* | *cuete* (Mex)
>
> **buzzed**
> *achispadito/a*
>
> **tipsy**
> *choborra*
> Scrambling syllables makes things cutesy and adds a wink-wink connotation, in this case conveying more affection and less judgment than *borracho*. It's not more or less drunk, it's just less pathetic.
>
> **well-done**
> *cocido/a* (S.Cone, Spn)

PARTY ALL WEEK!)))

SEMANALCOHÓLICA

Gluglunes	Glug-glug-glug
Mamartes	*Mamas*, you suck like a baby on a mammary.
Miercolitros	Liters and liters of the stuff
Juevebes	And you drink.
Beviernes	And you drink, all week, and on the weekend...
Sabadrink	...'et's haveadrink!
Dormingo	Sleep it off!

sloppy drunk
picado/a ("minced") | *taja* (Spn)

pickled
curado/a

wasted
fumigado/a (Mex) | *punto* (Spn)

Last night we all **got totally trashed**.
*Anoche todos **nos pusimos pedos**.* (LatAm) | *...**se agarró un pedo*** (S.Cone)
Pedo literally means "fart," and anything done *al pedo* is done pointlessly or blindly.

Last night we **went on a binge**.
*Anoche **fuimos de juerga fuimos de cuete** | **decuete*** (Mex)

We were drinking everything in sight.
Nos chupamos hasta el agua del inodoro.

I can't even remember **driving drunk**.
*Nisiquiera me acuerdo haber **conducido cuete**.* (Mex) | *...**manejado moña*** (Spn)

Sounds like a serious **bender**.
*Suena como **un vinagre** serio.* (Spn) | *...**una curda...*** (S.Cone)

·····The morning after
La mañana siguiente

Of course, all this cirrhosis-inducing drunkenness has its consequences.

I'm about to...
Estoy a punto de...

throw up
largar

puke
buitrear (CenAm, Andes, S.Cone)

projectile vomit
lanzar

pass out
desmayarme

I have a **splitting hangover**.
*Tengo una **cruda aguda**.* | *...un **guayabo agudo*** ("guava tree") (Andes)

He's/She's **hung over**.
*El/Ella está **crudo/a**.* (CenAm) | *...**enguayabado/a*** (Andes)

I got mean **dry-mouth** today.
*Hoy tengo una **secona** feroz.*

I got so drunk last night I **pissed the bed**.
Me emborraché tanto anoche que me meé en la cama.

Did we have sex last night?
¿Echamos algo anoche?

·····Cancersticks
Tubitos de cáncer

Tobacco may be persecuted in the First World, but when you stray off the beaten path in the tourist-loving Third World you'll find that people couldn't give a shit about secondhand smoke. Since, you know, they have to worry about other problems like famine and guerrilla warfare and whatnot. Whether you love the stuff or want cigarettes eradicated from our planet, here are the terms you'll need to know.

You sell **smokes**?
*¿Vendes **zafiros**?* (Mex)

Can you spare a **cig**?
*¿Te sobra un **faso**?* (S.Cone) | *...**fallo*** (Andes)

Not a single **cancerstick**?
*¿Ni un **cáncer**?*

Just one **drag**!
*¡Un **toque** nomás!* | *...**plon*** (Andes)

Not even from the **butt**?
*¿Nisiquiera del **pucho**?*

You're a fiend. You must **smoke like a chimney**.
*Eres un maniático. Debes **fumar como una chimenéa**.*

Yeah, **I chain-smoke** like a whore in the slammer.
*Sí, **fumo uno tras otro** como puta encarcelada.*

Could you stop **exhaling in my direction**?
*¿Podrías parar de **soplar por aquí**?*

·····Marijuana
Marejuancho

Spanish speakers have thousands of variants for talking about Mary Jane, from *mare-juancho* ("makes-Johnny-dizzy") to *mariguano* to *marihuan* to *mora* ("berry," the cutesy variant of the Mexican *mota*).

Weed
Mota (Mex)

Bud
La marimba (Andes)

The Herb
La hierba ; La hierbabuena

Hash
La grifa | El costo (Spn)

> **I'm feeling all hashed out.**
> *Me siento grifo del todo.*

Wanna smoke **a joint**?
*¿Quiéres fumarte **un pito**?*
Pito also means "tube" and "rod," so you can imagine the double entendres.

When are we gonna roll that **spliff**?
*¿Cuándo vamos a liar ese **canuto**?*

Toke that **roach**.
*Tóquete ese **puchito bacha**.* (Mex)

Should we **hotbox it**?
*¿Debemos **hornearlo**?*

Man, do I love **smokin' dope**.
*Corno me gusta **fumetear**.*

You look **nicely baked**.
*Te ves **bien fumado**.*

Nah, I'm just a bit **lightheaded**.
*Nada, es un toque de **la pálida**.*

Whatever, you're a **pothead**.
*Ni modo, eres un/una **fumero/a**.*

At least I'm not a **burnout**.
*Por lo menos no soy un/una **quemado/a**. (S.Cone)*

If you say so, **potheaderino**.
*Si tú lo dices, **Fumanchero/a**.*

·····Doped up
Puesto

Although much of America's hard drugs come from Latin
America, using the hard stuff is pretty rare in the developing
world, and none too openly discussed either, given the steep
penalties for possession in *any* quantity. Still, here's some
handy slang for substances people use to sully the temples
of their bodies.

Snort a bump.
Jalar *un toquito.*

Where can I score some…?
¿Dónde puedo conseguirme…?

> **pills**
> *pastis | chocho* (Mex)
>
> **coke**
> *perico | farlopa* (Spn) | *falopa* (S.Cone)
>
> **blow**
> *nieve* ("snow") ; *talco* ("talcum powder")
>
> **high-octane coke**
> *mosca* (Mex)

rock
piedra basuco (Andes)

a bag of "white" (coke)
una bolsita de "blanquito"

horse (heroin)
el caballo jaco (Spn)

roofies / nightynights / date-rape drugs
burundungas

ecstasy
éxtasis (Mex) | *tacha* (Mex) | *rola* (Carib)

You ain't nothing but a...
No eres más que un/una...

cokehead
angurri | *enfarlopado/a* (Spn)

horsehead
yonqui (Spn)

dope fiend
drogata

junky
tecato/a (Mex) | *falopero/a* (S.Cone) | *jincho/a* (Spn)

He's sweating like that 'cuz he's **kicking**.
*Suda así por **la malilla**.* (CenAm) | *...**el mono*** (Spn)

That shit must be good cuz that boy is **trippin'**.
*Debe ser bueno eso porque ese chico está **volando**. |
...**del otro lado*** (Carib, Spn)

Don't drink that beer! I think that scumbag tried **to roofy**
you.
*¡No tomes esa cerveza! Me parece que ese reo intentó
emburundangarte.*

·····Houses of ill repute
Casas libertinas

Prostitution, though technically illegal, is alive and well in
Latin America, God bless its liberal soul. Even if you're not
planning on hitting up any brothels in your travels, it never

hurts to know what they're called, particularly since these terms are often jokingly used to refer to a really bangin' party that has an awesome girl-to-guy ratio.

Who wants to go to a **cabaret**? (burlesque or dancing establishment)
*¿Quién quiere ir a un **cabaré**?*

Sure, as long as it's not a **crab-eret**. (no stage or dance floor, just a straight-up brothel)
*Bueno, con que no sea un **cabarute**.*

Could we compromise on a **gentlemen's club**?
*¿Y si transijamos en una **casa de idolatría**?*

Fine, let's roll to the **titty bar**.
*Vale, larguémonos al **antro de vicio**.*

Me too, I'm down for the **strip club**, but let's skip the **brothel**.
*Yo también, estoy listo para el **estripclub**, pero no para un **bordelo**.*

Seriously, I got crabs at the last **whorehouse**.
*En serio, me tocaron ladillas en la última **ramería**.*

Man, that's because that place was a **crackwhore-house**.
*Chavón, es porque ese lugar era una **chinchería**. | ...**piringundín** (S.Cone)*

·····Don't be a snitch!
¡No seas botón!

Unless your idea of tourism involves seeing the inside of a Third-World prison (not recommended), you may wanna study up on these important bywords for police presence.

Here come the...!
¡Viene/Vienen...!

po-po
la pole

cops
la cana | la tomba (Andes)

fuzz
los pacos (LatAm) | *la jura* (Mex)

pigs
los cuicos (Mex) | *los puercos* (Carib) | *los cobanis*
(S.Cone) | *los bolillos* (Col)

Hide your **stash**!
*¡Esconde el **clavo**!* (Mex) | *...la **clatera**!* (Andes)

Oh shit, they're using the **billy clubs**!
*¡Mierda, están usando las **porras**! | ...los **bolillos**!* (Andes,
S.Cone)

They're gonna put us *all* in **lockup**!
*¡Nos van a meter todos **en cana**!*

Damn, they **nabbed** Pookie and took him away **in cuffs**.
***Agarraron** a Pookie y se lo llevaron **engrillado**.*

He's gonna end up in **the joint**.
*Va a terminar él en **el bote**.*

Well, he best remember that **snitches get stitches**.
*Le convendría acordarse que **los batidores salen bien
batidos**.* (S.Cone)

CHAPTER 4

BODY SPANISH
CASTELLANO CORPORAL

·····Hey, Fatso!
¡Oye, Gordo!

Spanish speakers are pretty blunt when describing each other's physical characteristics. Someone with a big beard is called Beardy, someone shaped like a pear is called…Pear. A well-hung man like myself is called…. You get the point.

Hey…!
¡Oye…!

Bignose
Narigón/ona

Flatnose
Ñata
This often carries a potentially racist connotation of having native blood.

Mangaeyes
Focojos
Literally, "spotlight"

One-eye
Tuerto/a
To say "look the other way" in Spanish, you'd say *se hace tuerto*, which is pretty funny if you think about it.

One-arm
Manco/a
Saying *no es manco* ("he's not one-armed") about someone means they're handy

Bushybeard
Barbudo

Mick Jagger Mouth
Jetón/ona

Fatlips
Bembón/ona (LatAm)
Bembón refers to a racially West African "look" and/or puffy, swollen lips—be careful with either connotation.

Bigass
Nalgón/ona

Bigtits
Pechona | *Chichuda* (Mex)

Birthin' hips
Caderota

Fatbelly
Panzón/ona

Old Saggy (fem.)
Adelaida

·····The whole package
El paquete entero

Here are the standards to describe the people that float your boat. When traveling, be sure to pay attention to local terms for hot men and women, because every region of every Spanish-speaking country has its own unique words. A lot are based on local food vocabulary—*una torta, una manteca, un churro, un chile, una chilera…*

That girl **is hot**.
*Esa chica **está buena**. | ...**es maciza*** (Spn)

> She's a **stone fox**.
> *Es una **buenota**.*

> Your mom's a **ten**, buddy.
> *Tu vieja es **un cuero**, macho.*

> Your sister's a **cutey**.
> *Tu hermana es un **bizcocho**.* (Mex)

Is it weird to think that Steve Urkel is **a total hunk**?
*¿Es raro pensar que Steve Urkel es **un buenón total**?*

Ohmigod, there are, like, so many **hot guys** here.
*¡Epa, mira los tantos **papis** que hay por aquí! |
...**papuchos...*** (Mex)

I love men with **big guns**.
*Como quiero a los hombres con **brazos macizos**.*

Your little brother is **ripped**!
*¡Tu hermanito está **fornido**! | ...**mamado*** (Mex)
In the Southern Cone, *mamado* means drunk or permanently
brain-damaged by drinking.

Lookin' **slim**!
*¡Te ves **delgado/a**!*

Are you a swimmer? You've got a **good, toned build**.
*¿Nadas? Tienes un **buen lomo**.*

·····Fugly
Defeorme

Because sometimes you just gotta tell it like it is.

> Is it just me, or is Mary Kate kind of **formless**?
> *¿Solo lo parece a mí, o es Mary Kate un poco **amorfa**?*

> At least she's not **frumpy**.
> *Por lo menos no es **babosa**.*
> Literally, a "slug"

He's a little **chubby in the cheeks** for my tastes.
*Para mí, él es un poco **fofito en las mejillas**.*

What've you been eating, **tubby**?
¿Qué estás comiendo, fofo/a?

What a **lardass**!
¡Qué gordinflón/ona!

> Hey, don't start with me, **Pillsbury**.
> *Epa, no te metas conmigo, Michelin.*

Ugh, you want me to talk to that **hunchback**?
Ufa, ¿quieres que hable yo con ese/a jorobado/a?

Sorry, but I don't date **beanpoles**.
Disculpa, pero no salgo con palancones/onas.

Were you born **bowlegged**?
¿Naciste rengo/a?

> You're **walking like a cowboy**, chief.
> *Estás rengueando, jefe/a.*

You look like an **emaciated** P.O.W.
Pareces un/a prisionero/a enclenque. | ...tílico/a (Mex)

> I'm not into the whole **boniness** thing.
> *No me da por todo ese asunto de la flaquencia.*
> Flaquencia can also be used as a polite way to insinuate an
> eating disorder.

She's got a great body, but a **face like a cockatoo**.
Tiene buen carrocería, pero con cara de cacatúa.

·····Stylin'
Engalaneado

What good is your slammin' body if you're dressed in a
sack and haven't changed your drawers in six days? Here
are some handy phrases for describing the styled—or
inadequately styled, as the case may be.

> **He/She looks...**
> *El/Ella se ve...*
>
> > **fashionable**
> > *galano/a*

put-together
bien compuesto/a

well-tailored
a la tela

sharp
prolijo/a

preened
prolijito/a

O.C.D. (as in, your shoelaces match your belt,
bag, underwear, and eye shadow)
T.O.C. (trastorno obsessivo-compulsivo)

unkempt
descuidado/a

sloppy
desaliñado/a

threadbare
deshilachado/a

like **a real mess**
bien abandonado/a

·····Tits and ass
Tetas y culo

The Eskimos, it's said, developed over 100 words for snow
because they've been surrounded by the terrible, freezing
stuff every moment of their miserable lives. Ergo, Spanish
speakers must be up to their ears in sweet, delicious ass
because they have more ways to describe *booty* than the
ancient Greeks had gods.

You have a great **bust**.
*Tienes un **delantero** tremendo.*

Play with my...
Juega con mis...

You have beautiful...
Tienes unos/unas...hermosas.

Could I **motorboat** your…?
*¿Puedo **hacer trompetillas con** tus…?* (Mex)

> **breasts**
> *senos*

> **boobies**
> *bubis*

> **knockers**
> *globos*

> **titties**
> *chichis* (Mex)

> **tits**
> *tetas* (Andes) | *lolas* (S.Cone)

I'm in love with your…
Estoy enamorado de tu/tus…

> **derriere**
> *trasero*

> **butt**
> *fundillo* (S.Cone) | *poto* (Andes)

butt cheeks
nalgas | pompis (Mex)

ass
culo | traste (S.Cone)

ass crack
raya del culo

ass cheeks
ancas

Damn! Check out that **big-booty girl** with all that junk in the trunk!
*¡Puchal ¡Míralo todo el cargo que lleva esa **nalgona**!*

Your boyfriend is **totally assless**.
*Tu novio es **totalmente desnalgado**.* (Mex)

I love Latinas and their **big, thunderous ass cheeks**.
*Como me gustan las latinas con esas **ancotas temibles** que llevan.*

I prefer British girls with those **right-solid rumps**.
*A mí me da más por las inglesas, con esas **ancas bien sólidas**.*

Why do Japanese chicks all have those **superflat butts**?
*¿Por qué tienen todas las japonesas **esos fundillos de aspirina**?*
Ever looked at an aspirin pill?

•••••Spare tires
Llantas

People come in all shapes and sizes. Some are blessed with nice, tight abs. Others have stomachs that spill over their jeans like overyeasted dough. Although we can't harvest all the fatties to make candles and petroleum jelly out of their fat deposits, at least we can make up funny names for their humungous beer guts.

You sure have a soft **belly**.
*Tienes la **panza** muy suavecita.*

Man, your dad's really got a **beer gut**.
*¡Qué **guata** tiene tu viejo, hombre!* (S.Cone, Andes) |
...***botijón***... (CenAm)

Is that woman actually with child, or does she just have a
pregger-gut?
*¿Esa mujer está con hijo de verdad, o tiene el **bombo**
nomás?*

You gotta start working off that **spare tire**.
*Deberías liberarte de esa **llanta**.*
(LatAm)

What about your **muffin-top**?
*¿Y tu **bollito**?*
Bollo (bun) also has a lot of local
usages: *turd* in Colombia, *dyke* in
Spain, *vulva* in Cuba...

Nice **six-pack**! Do you work out?
*¡Linda **tabla de chocolate**!*
¿Haces ejercicios?

> Nah, these **washboard abs**
> just come natural.
> *Psh, este **estómago de
> lavadero** vino así.*

·····Piss and shit
Pis y mierda

Like most bodily functions in the Spanish-speaking world, the
acts of peeing and pooping aren't considered scandalous
enough to generate much eloquence or circumlocution.
Everyone poops, right? So why get all worked up about it?

> **I gotta...**
> *Necesito...*
>
> > **hit the john**
> > *irme al trono*
> >
> > **drain the lizard**
> > *achicar la verga*

take a piss
mear

mark some territory
poner la firma

take a shit
cagar

drop a **turd**
*depositar un **zurullo** | ...**sorete** (S.Cone)*

drop off a **dung delivery**
*dejar una **entrega de estiércol***

I...
Yo...

am constipated
estoy estreñido

have diarrhea
tengo una cursera

have the shits
tengo la cagadera

have the runs
tengo un chorrillo (Mex)

left skid marks on my drawers
dejé un sello en los calzones

I got drunk and **pissed myself**.
*Me emborraché hasta **mearme** todo.*

Wake up, before you **wet the bed**.
*Despiértate antes que **meas en la cama**.*

It smells awful. **Did you shit yourself?**
*¡Qué aliento! ¿**Te cagaste?***

·····Bodily fluids
Fluidos corporales

Spanish speakers don't actually have much slang for bodily
fluids. They're kind of nonchalant about them, unlike the

British, who think that the ridiculous word "bloody" is the worst thing you could ever say to a person. The lesson, as usual: Brits are weird.

Earwax
Cera en los oídos

Unplug your ears, jackass!
*¡**Sácate la vela de las orejas**, jil!*

Snot
Moco

I have a terrible **runny nose**.
*Tengo una **moquera** terrible.*

He **got the snot knocked out of him** in that accident.
***Se hizo moco** en ese accidente.*

That **little snot-nose** just ran off with my bike seat!
*¡Ese **mocoso** acaba de llevarse el asiento de mi bici!*

You have **eyeboogers**, you mouthbreather!
*¡Tienes **graña**, baboso!*

Your **pimples** are getting out of control.
*Tus **espinillas** se están desbordando.*

You need to **pop those zits** before your face explodes.
*Tienes que **apretarte esos granos** antes de que te explote la cara.*

Everyone **gets blackheads** now and then.
*A todos **nos salen granitos** de vez en cuando.*

Is that **drool**?
*¿Son **babos**?*

Don't **drool all over yourself**, that's my sister!
*¡No **te babees todo**, esa es mi hermana!*

To menstruate
Reglar

I have **menstrual cramps**.
*Tengo **los cólicos**.*

Her **monthly visitor** came.
*Le vino **la regla**.*

Aunt Flo is visiting.
Don Goyo está de visitas. (Carib)

Don't start with her, she's **on the rag** somethin' fierce.
*No metes pata, está **monstruando** bien serio.*

·····Other bodily functions
Otras funciones corporales

Saying my dad **snores** is an understatement; he's a sawmill!
*Decir que mi viejo **ronca** sería quedarse corto; ¡es un aserradero!*

I used to **grind my teeth** in my sleep.
*Antes **rechinaba los dientes** cuando dormía.*

I got **cramps** in my leg last night.
*Me agarraron **calambres** en las piernas anoche.*

Stand me up, I'm all **dizzy** from smoking so much pot.
*Párame, que estoy todo **mareado** de tanto fumetear.*

She's **preggers**.
*Está **encinta**.*

He put some bread in her oven.
Él le llenó la cocina de humo.
Literally, "He filled her kitchen with smoke"

·····Ailments
Achaques

If you're a true traveler to Latin America, you'll encounter plenty of spicy food, hard liquor, outdoor plumbing, and disease-carrying mosquitoes. Add 'em all up and chances are you're gonna get sick. But it all makes for a better story when you get home, so stop your sniveling and eat the worm already!

Move, I'm gonna…!
¡Múevete, que voy a…!

throw up
echar buitre (LatAm)

upchuck
buitrear (LatAm) | *trallar* (Spn)

hurl
guasquear (Andes) | *huacarear* (Mex)

How did I end up **covered in vomit**?
*¿Cómo terminé **cubierto en vómito**?*

He'll be **praying to the porcelain goddess** all night.
*Va a pasarse la noche **devolviendo atenciones**.*
Literally, "writing thank-you cards"

I have a **migraine**, get me a **painkiller**!
*¡Tengo **jaqueca**, alcánzame un **calmante**!*

I think I got **scabies** from sleeping in that creep's bed!
*¡Me parece que me tocó **la sarna** durmiendo en la cama de ese reo!*

I have **stomach cramps** from eating all that meat.
*Tengo **retortijones** por comer tanta carne.*

He's got **a bit of a gimpy leg**, right?
*Tiene **la pierna medio coja**, ¿verdad?*

Is he still **walking with a limp**?
*¿Sigue **cojeando**?*

CHAPTER 5

HORNY SPANISH
ESPAÑOL ARRECHO

Despite the Catholic heritage, sex is a big part of Spanish culture. Newsstands sell hardcore porno next to kids' comics, websites rank proudly the best sexual catcalls, and newscasters tend to be big-titted, raven-haired vamps that make Katie Couric look like a sexless, albino sloth. Because Spanish speakers are so down with sex, they don't demonize it the way Americans can. They have "natural," not illegitimate, children; tell "green" jokes instead of dirty ones; become "green" old men instead of dirty old ones; and have extramarital "adventures" instead of affairs. Not bad, considering that in most Spanish-speaking countries, divorce wasn't even legal 20 years ago.

•••••Fucking 101
Coger 101

There is no universal Spanish term for fucking. Spaniards use *joder* and Mexicans use *chingar,* both of which mean "to fuck" in those countries but "to irritate" everywhere else. The rest of Latin America uses *coger*. But Spaniards never got the memo and still use *coger* in its dictionary sense of "to catch, get, or hold." This causes mass hysteria among Latin Americans whenever they hear a Spaniard talking about needing to fuck a bus. To add to the confusion, *trincar* has the opposite problem and means "to seize or grab" everywhere except for Spain where, inevitably, it means "to fuck." You might wanna draw yourself a little chart at the airport.

I wanna...
Quiero...

Do you want to...?
¿Quieres...?

Let's go and...
Vámonos a...

I'd love to...
Me gustaría...

> **fuck**
> *coger* | *chingar* (Mex) | *follar* (Spn)
>
> **screw**
> *culear* | *fifar* (S.Cone)
>
> **boink**
> *tirar* (literally, "throw") | *curtir* (S.Cone)
>
> **knob**
> *empomar*
>
> **bone**
> *joder*
> *Joder*, like the British "bugger," can mean anything from mild, nagging irritation to sodomy. Most of the time it hovers ambiguously in between.
>
> **plug her**
> *enchufarla* (Mex)
>
> **hit that**
> *comérsela* | *dar masa* (Andes)
>
> **nail that ass**
> *clavar ese culo*

have a fuck
echar un palo

have a double-fuck
echar un doble-palo

have a fuckathon
echar un buen caldo
Ever made broth (*caldo*) from scratch? It takes all day.

have a quickie
echar un rapidín ; un cuiqui

get your rocks off
echar un polvo ("toss some powder") | *un talco*
(S.Cone)

leave it raw
fregarla (literally, "to scrub it") | *cepillarla* (literally,
"to scrub it with a cleaning brush")

hook up
ligar

pick someone up
levantarse a alguien

get involved with someone (sexually)
meterse con alguien

BURY THE BONE)))

HUNDIR EL HUESO

Fritar la berenjena	Deep-fry the eggplant
Engrasar la nutria	Grease the marmot
Enhebrar el hilo	Thread the needle (i.e., anally)
Enterrar la batata	Bury the yam
Medir el aceite	Dunk the dipstick
Revolver el estofado	Stir the coals
Serruchar el piso	Saw the floor
Peinar para adentro	Comb it from the inside
Ñaca-ñaca	Hubba-hubba
Frike-frike	Freaky-freaky
Dunga-dunga	Humpy-humpy

WHAT'S YOUR FAVORITE POSITION?)))

¿CUÁL ES TU POSICIÓN FAVORITA?

Missionary	*Misionero*
Doggy-style	*La adoración*
Cowgirl	*Cabalgando*
Wheelbarrow	*La gran carretilla*
Standing T	*El cartero* ("the postman"!)
Spoon	*En caja*
Reverse cowgirl	*Cabalgando hacia atrás*
Both knees up	*La defensa amorosa*
Both legs up	*El candelabro*
Ankles on giver's shoulders	*Los abdominales* (an abs workout!)
Knees held spread	*El barco de vela* ("the galley")
Spoonee turned halfway back	*La santanderina*

·····Gettin' horny
Arrechándose

A word should capture the essence of the thing it stands for. "Butterfly," for instance, sounds soft, fluttery, and beautiful. "Dump" sounds like a stinky, formless mound of crap. So you'd think that the word for orgasming would be something like "amazingawesomebestfeelingeverIloveitsomuchIwantto marryit." This isn't the case in English, though, where formal sex talk consists of excruciating words like "ejaculate" and "climax" that sound like they're about as much fun as getting your genitals clamped in a vise. Spanish, on the other hand, uses lyrical, poetic phrases like "boil over," "outdo yourself," and "go into a frenzy" that capture the true spirit of busting a nut.

Damn, girl, you're getting me **all excited**.
*Ufa, chica, me estás dando **un buen morbo**.* (Spn)

You make me so **horny**.
*Me pones tan **arrecho/a**.* (LatAm)

I got **a boner that won't quit**.
*Tengo **un duro que dura**.*

I'm hard for you.
Estoy al palo para ti.

I want it **inside me**.
*Lo quiero **adentro**.*

Why don't we do it right here?
*¿**Por qué no lo echámos** aquí nomás?*

Oh, you **feel so good**.
*Ooo, **estás bueno**.*

You're **so big and hard**.
*Estás **tan duro y grandón**.*

Wow, you're **really wet** today.
*¡Wow, qué estás **bien húmeda** hoy!*

You're **makin' soup in my panties**!
*¡Me estás **calentando la estufa**!*
Literally, "stoking the stove"

Come on, **faster**! **Harder**!
*¡Dale, **más rápido**! ¡**Más fuerte**!*

Are you close to **cumming**?
*¿Estás por **correrte**?*
Literally, "to run, flow, or brim over"

Ohmigod, I'm gonna **cum**!
*¡Carajo, me estoy por **llegar**!*

Cum on my face.
***Lechéame** la cara.*

Oh yeah, **take it all**, you freak!
*¡Ja, **tómalo todo**, loca!*

·····Other sex acts
Otros actos sexuales

Variety is the spice of life. All good things in moderation. Man cannot live on genital sex alone. Sometimes he needs a blowjob or a good circlejerk to balance his yin and yang.

Will you suck me off?
¿Me lo chuparías?

Wanna **blow me**?
*¿Quisieras **mamármelo**?*

I like it when **you swallow** my cum.
*Me gusta cuando te **tragas** la leche.*

I want you **to ride me** like a pony.
*Quiero que **me cabalgues** como una yegua.*

C'mon, just give me one **dick-poke**.
*Dale, déme un **puntazo** nomás.*

If you don't have a condom, just **skeet-shoot** all over me.
*Si no hay condones, **dispárame en blanco** nomás.*

Pull out at the last minute and **splash it on** my tits.
*Al fin, **ponla en marcha atrás** y **salpícame** las tetas.*

I'd like to try…
Quisiera probar…

How 'bout…?
¿Qué tal…?

Have you ever done…?
¿Has echo alguna vez…?

>**dry-humping**
>*la frottage* (from the French)

>**a blowjob**
>*una mamada | un pete* (S.Cone)

>**a full-service blowjob**
>*recitar el rosario*

>**a handjob**
>*la paja* (LatAm)
>Literally, "tumbleweed"

YOU SAY "FRENCH KISS," I SAY "RUSSIAN ANAL MASSAGE")))

For some reason, Spanish speakers have decided that certain nationalities are better than others at performing specific sex acts. How do they know, for instance, that the Lebanese give the world's best armpitjobs or that no one can massage an asshole like a Russian? Only the most seasoned sex tourist would know, and I'm guessing he's a native speaker.

HACER...	GIVE A/HAVE A...
una francesa	blowjob
un tailandés	full-body boob massage
un croata	full-body lickdown
un serbio	full-body chompdown
un árabe	face-sitting (female on male)
un ruso	anal massage
un griego	anal sex
un romano	orgy
un japonés	floor sex (with pillows for props)
un turco	sex with recipient cuffed behind back
un libanés	armpitjob
una cubana	titfuck
una pinza birmana	footjob (literally, a "Burmese grip")

a circlejerk
una carrera de pajas (LatAm)
Literally, "jackoff race"

a circlesuck
una margarita

a sex party
el partus ; una "fiesta"

69
sesenta y nueve

backdoor action
la trastienda
Literally, "backdoor shop"

cunnilingus
el buceo
Literally, "diving"

a snowball
un beso blanco

a rimjob
un beso negro

the ol' finger in the butt
la espada de Carlomagno
Isn't "Sword of Charlemagne" more fun to say than "finger in the butt"?

a golden shower
una lluvia dorada

·····Nuts and bolts
Tornillos y tuercas

Unless you're gonna be a doctor, you should probably expand your selection of sex nouns beyond the medical ones you learned in school. I wish there was space to convey the astounding richness of regional and poetic variations, but alas, a guide is not the same as an encyclopedia, which is what we'd end up with if I tried to include all the thousands of Spanish names for "junk."

Grab my...
Agárrame...

Play with my...
Manotéame...

Suck my...
Chúpame...

Touch my...
Tócame...

You have huge/a huge...
Tienes muy grande/tienes un/a grande...

privates
los agentes

package
el paquete | *el bulto* ("bundle")

nuts
las bolas | *los belines* (S.Cone)

balls
los huevos (Mex) | *los cojones* (Spn)

'nads
las pelotas (S.Cone)

boner
la puntada

dick
el pito

cock
la verga

rod
el pijo | *la pija* (S.Cone) | *la polla* (Spn)

shaft
la pinga | *la poronga* (S.Cone)

DiCK-TALK)))

JERGA VERGA

Treetrunk	*El tronco*
Soup can	*El marlo* (lit., "corncob")
One-eyed giant	*El chino tuerto* ("slanted eye" = urethra)
Baldy	*El pelado*
The hose	*La manguera*
The meatstick	*La butifarra, morcilla*
The stickshift	*La palanca*
Piece	*El pedazo*
Knob	*El pomo*
Limpdick	*Un pene de soga*
Little dick	*El cacahuete ; el maní* (lit., "peanut")

·····'Gina talk
Chochisme

Lick my…
Lámeme…

Hit my…
Méchame…

Eat my…
Cómete…

Shave my…
Aféitame…

Manhandle my…
Manotéame…

> **pussy**
> *la chocha*
> The only place *chocha* doesn't mean "pussy" is in Argentina, where it's used as an adjective to mean "stoked"!
>
> **carpet**
> *la alfombrita ; el felpudo* ("the felted bit")
>
> **bush**
> *el arbusto ; la selvita* ("the little jungle")
>
> **box**
> *la pandorca* (Carib)
>
> **peach**
> *la castaña* ("chestnut")
>
> **clam**
> *la almeja*
>
> **cooch**
> *la chucha* (Andes)
>
> **poontang**
> *la concha* ("conch shell") (S.Cone) | *la panocha* (Carib)
>
> **cunt**
> *el funciete* (Mex) | *el coño* (Spn)
> Spaniards also use *coño* as an expletive like "fuck!" or "shit!"

shaved pussy
la chocha afeitadita | *la chocha rasurada* (Mex) | *la concha rapada* (S.Cone)

clit
la campana ("bell") ; *el botón* ("the button")

G-spot
el punto G

cameltoe
el hachazo

perineum
el periné

·····Accessories
Accesorios

Sex today seems to involve all sorts of preparation and specialized equipment. Gone are the good ol' days when you just dragged your smelly ass down to the next hut, fucked like cavemen, and had a baby nine months later that probably died of hypothermia. Now you gotta have perfume, satin sheets, birth control, a Barry White album, a mirror on the ceiling, at least 10 minutes of foreplay, and a vibrator for reinforcement.

Are you on **the pill**?
*¿Estás tomando **la píldora**?*

Man, I miss my ex, who had an **IUD**.
*Como echo a menos a la equis que tenía "**DIU**". ; ...**La "T"** ; ...**El ancla*** (literally, "the anchor")

Do you have…?
¿Tienes…?

a condom
un preservativo

a rubber
un impermeable | *un forro* (S.Cone)

any piercings
perforaciones

an STD
una venérea
You can also use this to call someone "a walking STD!"

Reach me a...
Alcánzame un/una...

Wanna try a...?
¿Quisieras probar con un/una...?

I love using a...
Me encanta usar un/una...

dildo
consolador
Consolador literally means "consolation," like for not having dick on hand when you want it!

vibrator
vibrador

tickling cockring
párpado de carba
This glorious phrase literally connotes the eyelashes of a goat. Isn't Spanish awesome!

blindfold
venda

gag
mordaza

paddle
paleta

•••••Sexual sociology
La sociología sexual

It's a well-known fact that when a guy sleeps around he's a ladies' man, but if a girl gets around she ain't nothing but a slut. This double standard exists all over the world and goes to show you that, deserved or not, your sex life often comes to define you. Maybe that explains why so many homophobes are secretly gay themselves.

That **horndog** would fuck anything on legs.
*Esa **cachonda** cojería cualquier cosa con piernas*
Literally, "bitch in heat"

Too bad he's an **impotent**.
*Qué lástima que es un **deficiente sexual**.*

That **sterile dude** couldn't get you pregnant with emotion.
*Ese **huevo duro** no te podría impregnar ni con el amor de Diòs.*

She keeps cheating on her **cuckold** of a husband.
*Ella le sigue engañando al **cornudo** de su marido.*
This is one of the most common and severe insults in Hispanic culture. It means you've been cheated on and made a fool of, and is frequently insinuated by making the devil horns sign with your hand and bumping it against your temple.

Stop **making a cuckold of** my brother!
*¡Basta de **ponerle los cuernos a** mi hermano!*

Careful, he's **a ladies' man** and **a swinger** to boot.
*Ojo, que es **un mujeriego** y en cima **un partusero**.*

He's always **sleeping around**.
*Siempre **anda culeando**.*

Quit humping my thigh, you **creep**.
*Basta de chocarme el muslo, **avión**.*

That **cocksucker** cheated on me with my sister.
*Ese **mamavergas** me fue infiel con mi hermana.*

You'll never get your rocks off with that **dicktease**.
*Nunca vayas a echar un polvo con esa **calientapijas**.*

Your girlfiend is **frigid**.
*Tu novia es una **chuchafría**.* (Andes) | *...**coñofrío*** (Spn)

That **easy slut**'s got a **quick-action pussy**.
*Esa **culopronto** tiene una **concha de lata**.*
Yes, *concha de lata* does mean "aluminum pussy." Why? Because aluminum gets hot in seconds flat, that's why.

I wouldn't date **a loose girl** like her.
*Yo no me metería con **una flojona** como ella.* | *...**una conchuda**...* (S.Cone)

I wouldn't fuck that **hussy** with *your* dick.
*A esa **zorra** no le metería ni la verga* tuya.

She looks like **a virgin** but I think she just **plays innocent**.
*Ella se parece **invicta** pero yo pienso que **se hace la inocente** nomás.*

They're just a big **circle of fuckbuddies**.
*Son un gran **enjambre mongol**.*
Literally, "Mongolian herd"

CHAPTER 6

ANGRY SPANISH
ESPAÑOL ENCABRONADO

Cursing in Hispanic cultures is a hugely popular, over-the-top form of poetry. Friends spar against each other like mortal enemies, gossips interrupt their narratives to unleash bucolic torrents of abuse on innocent passersby, and taxi drivers with little hope of a tip will spend five whole minutes roundly cursing a fellow driver. It's a way of life, a whole grammar of embellishment. Study up—or you might never fit in.

•••••Pissed off
Encabronado

Latins aren't more hot-blooded than other peoples, they're just more open and expressive about life's little murderous rages.

Fucking wetback beaners...
Frijoleros mojados...
Google the music video *Frijolero*, by Mexican rock supergroup Molotov, to get a feel for how offensive this term is.

Racist Republicans...
Republicanos migra...

Euro-mullets…
Esas melenas de gallego fofo (LatAm)… | Esas melenas de futbolista sudaca (Spn)…

> **make me angry**
> *me enojan*

> **tick me off**
> *me ponen del hígado*

> **piss me off**
> *me encabronan*

> **get on my nerves**
> *me ponen de los nervios*

> **really bother me**
> *me molestan seriamente*

> **annoy the hell out of me**
> *me fastidian hasta la madre*

Get away from me!
¡Lárgate!

Leave me alone.
Déjame en paz.

I'm about to lose my shit.
Estoy perdiendo mi puto quicio.

Keep **cussin' me out** and I'm gonna **snap** any second.
*Sigue **puteándome** y en cualquier momento voy a **soltar la rabia**.*
Somehow, "unleash the fury" (*soltar la rabia*) sounds less hokey in Spanish.

▪▪▪▪▪Don't be stupid
No seas gil

The most basic and prolific Spanish insult is an attack on one's intelligence. Scholars suggest that Hispanics have so many words for stupidity because they have childlike minds and are insecure about their mental capacity. To that we say: "Takes one to know one, Mr. Smartypants Poopybreath!"

You're **kinda stupid**, aren't you?
*Eres **medio tontito/a**, ¿no?*

Were you born this **slow**, or did that just happen recently?
*¿Naciste **lento/a**, o pasó recién?*

The kid's got **rocks for brains**. He's **totally out to lunch**.
*Este chico tiene **piedras por sesos**. Es **totalmente lelo**.*

Don't be such a...
No seas...

He's/She's a complete...
El/Ella es un...completo.

That fat American is a flat-out...
Ese/a yanqui gordo/a es un/una...pleno.

dummy
gil
You can dress this one up as *un flor de gil*, which translates to "a royal dumbass."

dumbass
gilún
When dumbasses travel in packs, you can refer to the herd as *una gilada*, or "a bunch of dumbasses."

dumbfuck
gilazo | gilipollas (Spn)

bag of rocks
maleta

doofus
buey
Literally, "ox"

blockhead
adoquín | cuadrado/a (S.Cone)

serious scatterbrain
pasmado/a

moron
mamerto/a | panoli (Spn)

nitwit / dimwit / halfwit
baboso/a ; atarantado/a ; tarado/a

SCOReS OF WHOReS)))

PUTEANDO A LAS PUTAS

Spanish has so many words for actual sex workers that, over time, half of them have become semi-benign terms used for slutty amateurs and ex-girlfriends you're not even mad at.

Bitch	*Puta*
Tramp	*Mujerzuela*
Skank	*Una macarra* (*un macarra* is a pimp!)
Slut	*Pelandusca* | *cuero* (Carib, Andes)
Ho	*Hortera* | *gata* (S.Cone)
Hoochie	*Una guarra* | *un yiro* (S.Cone)
Whore	*Zorra* | *jinetera* (Mex, Carib)
Hooker	*Fulana* (also means "random girl"), *Pendón* (Spn)
Trick	*Furcia* | *lumi* (Spn)
Prostitute	*Ramera* | *guaricha* (Andes)

retard
retardado/a

mental deficient
infradotado/a

mongoloid
mogólico/a \| *oligofrénico/a* (S.Cone)

·····Talkin' 'bout yo' mama
Mentándote la madre

When you're ready to take the confrontation out of first gear, try out one of the following aspersions on someone's character or heritage. They're guaranteed to bring on a case of what Spanish speakers call *mala sangre*. Remember to tuck your chin before you get punched in the face.

You're nothing but a...
No eres nada sino un/una...

You're no better than a two-bit, scummy...
Eres tan ruin, mezquino/a...

My cheating excuse for a husband is a real...
El canalla engañador de mi marido es un/una...de veras.

What a...!
¡Qué...!

> **sunnuvabitch**
> *hijueputa ; 'jueputa*
>
> **sunnbitch**
> *jonutas | juepuchas* (S.Cone)
>
> **son of a royal old bitch**
> *hijo de la gran puta vieja*
>
> **creep**
> *desgraciado/a*
>
> **piece of trash**
> *basura*
>
> **abomination**
> *aborto*
> Literally, "abortion"
>
> **born asshole**
> *malparido*
> Literally, "badly born" or "miscarriage that survived"
>
> **plague**
> *peste*
>
> **vermin**
> *insecto*
>
> **worm**
> *larva*

·····Go to hell
Véte al carajo

The purest Spanish curses tell their recipients to get lost, then offer an activity for them to do once they're gone. That activity usually involves being killed, anally penetrated, or covered in the vaginal secretions of their mother (you know, the usual).

Clear out! Scram!
¡Corta campo! ¡Rájate!

Go fly a kite.
Vete a espulgar un galgo.
Literally, "go de-flea a greyhound"

Go to hell!
¡Ándate bien al carajo!

Go wipe your ass!
¡Ánda a limpiarte el culo!

Don't set foot in here again or I'll put you in a cast lickety-split.
No vuelves a poner pie aquí *o te lo pongo en un yeso rapidingo.*

Oh, **go spank your monkey**, you useless son of a bitch!
*¡Ánda, **hazte una manuela**, hijueputa inútil!*

Go to hell and **put a finger in your ass** when you get there!
*¡Véte al diablo y **métete el dedo en el ojete** cuando llegues!*

Why don't **you go give yourself a good enema**?
*¿Por qué no **te vas a hacerte una buena enema**?*

Why don't you take that billy club and **go fuck yourself with it**?
*¿Por qué no te llevas ese bolillo y **te lo metes en el culo**?*

Go try your bullshit on the hooker that spawned you!
*¡**Ándate a cantar tus pavadas** a la ramera que te parió!*

Go knock on the tired poontang of the hoochie you call a mom!
*¡**Rájate, que claves en la recalcada chocha** de la gata que llamas mami!*

Go to the rotten cunt of your whore mother!
*¡**Vete al coño podrido** de tu puta madre!*

·····Talkin' shit
Diciendo cagadas

Spanish speakers inherited the Roman obsession with poop, or specifically, the idea that a civilization should be judged by the sophistication of its plumbing. This is a big deal in Spanish since Latin Americans, as descendants of indigenous peoples, are *very* insecure about being considered "civilized." This is why the strongest cussword in Spanish is not "fuck" or "cunt," but "to shit." And the most dramatic form of shitting (and the mother of all Spanish insults) is to shit on one's enemies.

I shit on…!
¡Me cago en…!

my old man and his stupid curfew
mi viejo y su queda idiota

crooked-ass Customs—let them fleece the next guy
la aduana chingona—que chinguen al próximo

the Host [of the Eucharist]
la hostia
This anti-Catholic expletive refers to the toiletbowl-like gesture made by the cupped hands of the priest administering the Eucharist.

the head of Benito Juárez
la cabeza de Benito Juárez
You might hear fervent Catholics uttering this one, as Benito Juárez is still detested in the God-fearing world for promoting secularism.

the ridiculous toupee of Petey Wilson
el peluquín ridículo de Piti Wilson
Pete Wilson was formerly California's governor and chief supporter of Proposition 187, which stripped illegal immigrants of government services and basic human rights. He's still reviled among U.S. Latinos.

my idiot of a president
el idiota de mi presidente

your **mongoloid whore of a mother for having
birthed you**
la puta mogólica de tu mamá por haberte partido

I shit on your mother's torn-up, whoring cunt!
¡Me cago en el coño reventado de tu madre ramera!
The H-bomb of all Spanish curses.

·····Fightin' words
Palabras peladas

The best part of any barfight is the moment just before fists
start flying, when the two dudes are talking about all the
nasty things they're going to do to each other and how hard
they're gonna fuck each other up. It's so homoerotic that
you're not sure if they're gonna fight each other or just gonna
start fucking right there on the bar.

I'm gonna **tie** you **in knots**.
*Te voy a **atar en nudos**.*

Take it easy, I don't wanna have to **knock you to pieces**.
*Tómala con calma, no quiero tener que **reventarte**.*

You're gonna get **ripped to shreds**!
*¡Te va a dejar **harapiento**!*

I'm gonna crack that hollow gourd of yours in half!
*¡**Te voy a partir** esa calabaza vacua!*

I'm gonna **open a can of whoop-ass** you won't soon
forget!
*¡Te voy a **dar una paliza** de recuerdo!*

Keep givin' me the stinkeye and I'm gonna **make
mincemeat** out of you!
*¡Sigue con la ojeriza y te voy a **hacer polvo**!*

He's gonna **whoop** me **like an eggbeater**!
*¡Me va a **batir como la crema para la torta**!*

I'm gonna **mop the floor with your hideous face**, you
mongoloid!
*¡Te voy a **usar la cara espantosa como trapo de piso**,
mogólico!*

I'm gonna **fuck** you **up royally**!
*¡Te voy a **hacer una mierda líquida**!*
Literally, "I'm gonna make liquid shit out of you."

I'm gonna **go medieval on your ass**!
*¡Voy a **practicar el medioevo con tu culo**!*

Spread your cheeks cuz I'm 'bout to **leave your asshole looking like the Holland Tunnel**!
*¡**Ábrete las cachas** porque estoy a punto de **dejarte el ojete como el túnel de Holland**!*

·····Punches and kicks
Golpes y patadas

The great thing about Spanish is the precision afforded by its suffixes, perhaps the coolest of which is "*-azo*." When added to the end of a noun it basically means "the act of being smacked by (that noun)." So if your girlfriend throws dishes at you and lands one, it's *un platazo*, if you throw the cat right back at her it's *un gatazo*, if the wall crashes on her it's *un paredazo*, and so on.

Did you see that **punch**?
*¿Viste ese **puñetazo**?*

He **smacked** him good.
*Le **zumbó** bien.* | *...**sonó**...* (Mex)

I'm gonna **haul off and deck you** if you don't shut your mouth.
*Te voy a **dar una paliza súbita** si no te callas la boca.*
La paliza súbita, "the sudden whoop-ass," can refer to a hurricane or just an unexpected and devastating swat to the back of the head, particularly from a parent.

She **broke his nose** with that **bitchslap**.
*Le **rompió la nariz** con ese **cachetazo**.*

I **backhanded** that fool and gave him a **black eye**.
*A ese gilazo le dí **un sopapo trasero** y le dejé con un **ojo morado**.*

You **slap** like a girl.
*Das **guantazos** como una nena.*
Literally, "glove-slaps," like for a duel!

I'm gonna **uppercut** your face.
*Te voy a **dar un ganchazo** en la cara.*

I'll **karate chop** you in the neck.
*Te voy a **dar un hachazo de karate** en el cuello.*

Kick him in the nuts!
*¡**Patéale** en los huevos!*

Put him in a **headlock**!
*¡Ponle en una **llave de cabeza**!*

Did you see that?! She picked him and **put him in a pile driver**!
*¿Viste eso? ¡Lo agarró y **le hizo el martinete**!*

·····Chill out
Cálmate

If you ever find yourself in a Latin American shanty town without a police squadron of protection, you may want to hide the trendy digital camera and start memorizing some of these phrases.

Can't we all just **get along**?
*¿No podríamos **llevarnos bien** nomás?*

Quit it, boys, break it up.
Basta, chicos, déjenlo.

Take it outside.
Llévalo afuera.

Calm the fuck down!
¡Cálmense, carajo!

Don't flip out!
!No flipes!

Slow down, tough guy.
Frénalo un poco, macho.

Just **forget about it**.
Olvídalo nomás.

It's not worth it.
No vale la pena.

Let's all just take it easy.
Tómenlo con calma.

Make love, not war.
Haz el amor, no la guerra.

Who wants a **group hug**?
*¿Quién quiere un **abrazo comunal**?*

CHAPTER 7

POPPY SPANISH
ESPAÑOL "POP"

Uncle Sam might like to think of everyone south of the border as a rustic farmhand sleeping against a cactus or lagging behind a *burro*, but Latin Americans are a lot more tech- and media-savvy than most of the Third World. Whether downloading bootleg DVDs, sending dirty text messages to a mistress, skyping to friends abroad, or bumping tunes from an off-brand MP3 player, the Spanish-speaker of the 21st century is a real media multitasker. So don't hold it against me if it takes you more than this chapter to catch up.

•••••The TV
La tele

Keep **channel surfing** and I'm gonna shove **the remote** up your ass.
*Sigue **haciendo zapping** y voy a meterte **el remoto** en el ojete.*

What's on TV?
¿Qué hay en la tele?

Sábado Gigante

This kitschy hodgepodge of game show, talk show, children's show, and sketch comedy was filmed live for eight straight hours every Saturday for 24 years in Chile—and in Miami for 21 years since. All that time, it's been synonymous with its charismatic host, "Don Francisco." All over Latin America and in the Latino U.S., Don Francisco is a household name whose show generally rates higher than any locally produced competition.

ShowMatch

Argentina's top-rated variety show continually morphs genres to hold down its top-rated spot, phasing in and out new formats (mini-gameshows, sketch comedy miniseries, and so on). In between new ideas, though, they stick to classics, like getting comedian Yayo (Adam Sandler meets Howard Stern) to offend starlets with dirty jokes, and following the ensuing confrontations and offstage hissyfits with a handheld camera, Jerry Springer–style.

Los Conquistadores del Fin del Mundo

The survival reality subgenre has been huge in Latin America. The biggest of the bunch have been *Expedición Crusoe* (the same as our *Survivor*) and *Los Conquistadores del Fin del Mundo* (similar to *The Amazing Race*). Filmed in the Argentine Patagonia, contestants on *Conquistadores* race to the famous "End of the World Lighthouse" in Ushuaia. There's even an edition in which only pureblooded Basques can compete!

Cantando/Bailando por un Sueño (Mexico and Argentina)

Like *Dancing with the Stars*, professional singers or dancers pair up with a celebrity of the opposite sex to sing or dance a duet. But since the Mexican version blew up the charts by substituting singing for dancing, Argentina had to up the ante. It chose to take the format in a strange and tacky new direction: ice-skating with the stars. A musical-comedy version of *Cantando por...* is in the works, as well as a spin-off devoted to (I kid you not) competitive swimming.

Kassandra

This Venezuelan soap powerhouse about a gypsy marrying into money holds the Guinness record for most exported Spanish-language television show, with 128 countries having picked it up. During its bloody civil war, Serbia was one of these 128. Curiously, the daily cease-fire in Sarajevo coincided with the hour *Kassandra* aired. Coincidence?

Miramar

To Mexicans, *Miramar* was just another vendetta-filled *telenovela* about a working-class girl, her Prince Charming, and the backbiting bitches in the prince's family. But when it was broadcast during Ramadan of 1997, it caused such a sensation that a council of Muslim clerics in Abidjan, worried about the show's runaway popularity, actually rescheduled evening prayers to keep up mosque attendance!

Los Hombres de Paco

This cop-drama about a somewhat incompetent trio of idiot cops is currently Spain's top-rated fiction show, even though it has heapings of black-comedy and social commentary, two things notoriously absent from American primetime.

·····The movies
Las pelis

Usually, the names of American movies are given direct Spanish translations when they're released abroad. But the monolingual lackeys who slave away in studio think tanks occasionally decide on titles that make those online translation websites look graceful: *101 Dalmations* nonsensically became "Night of the Cold Noses," *Mrs. Doubtfire* turned into the saccharine "Your Daddy Forever," and *Brokeback Mountain* was given a title that I'm pretty sure was stolen from a Hardy Boys novel: "The Secret in the Mountain."

> Let's go see a...**on the big screen**.
> *Vamonos a ver un/una...**en pantalla grande**.*

How long has that…**been running**?
*¿Desde cuándo **está en cartel** ese/esa…?*

tearjerker
lacrimógena

cartoon
dibujo animado

screwball comedy
comedia blanca

meathead movie
película machote

chick flick
peli melosa

feel-good hit of the year
éxito sensacional de optimismo ligero

documentary
documental

B movie
película "serie B"

porno
porno

·····Comics
Los cómics

Comics are *huge* in the Spanish-speaking world—people of all walks of life read cheap comics in a whole range of genres that we simply don't have here. Granny flips through her B&W soap-operas, Gramps mutters into his bound anthology of yesteryear's political cartoons, the goth kid next to you chuckles into his true-crime slasher, the hormone-case across the aisle isn't trying hard enough to hide the boner his girly comic is giving him. Even the pamphlets that Jehovah's Witnesseses put in your hand are surprisingly stylish bits of comic art!

Where are your…?
¿Dónde tiene usted las…?

Are this week's… in?
¿Ya tienes las…de esta semana?

comic strips (typically sold in anthologies)
tiras cómicas

political cartoons (single-frame political comics)
viñetas políticas

comic books
historietas | *tebeos* (Spn) | *moneros* (Mex)

soap-opera comics
comics sentimentales

kids' comics
comics infantiles

Japanese comics
comics manga (never conjugated)

·····Pop music
Música "pop"

Pop music and ghetto music have been all but synonymous in Latin America since long before gangster rap turned suburban malls into a carnival of white-kid posturing. These are the hotter currents in Spanish-speaking pop music nowadays, for better or for worse.

Let's listen to some…
Pónnos algo de…

Bump that…
Súbele a esa…

I can't stand…
No soporto…

Norteñas
Nortenas are border songs, ballads about *coyotes* (people-smugglers) and *narqueros* (drug-smugglers) set to an evolved *Banda* (border-country) tune that's lighter on the polka backbeat. Imagine Garth Brooks doing uptempo, happy-dance covers of gangster-rap songs with an accordion.

Cumbia
This term refers to a whole family of pop genres including everything from saccharine singalongs to Timberlakey pop to dance-party jams, all featuring an Andean blend of catchy hooks; solid, danceable backbeats; and melodies even a drunk could follow. The lyrics tend to be salt-of-the-earth, the instrumentation jangly and keyboardy, and the clubs where it's DJ'ed insipid and Budweiser-esque. But even at its worst, *cumbia* is like a good wedding band: functional for everyone, irritating to no one.

Reggaetón
Around the time Shaggy and Sean Paul were bringing Jamaican "Dancehall" to the U.S., pop stars like Tego Calderón, Don Omar, and Calle 13 (think Jay-Z, 50 Cent, and Ludacris, respectively) started adapting the genre to the palates of Latin American listeners. The production is less smoked-out than its Jamaican cousin, with lyrics closer to top-40 hip-hop than gangsta rap or Jamaica's terrifying fagbash subgenre.

Perreo
This Puerto Rican predecessor to *Reggaetón* has all but disappeared into the dustbin of pop music history. However, the name ("doggy-business") is still used to

refer to hardcore bumping and grinding or *sexo vestido*
("sex with clothing on").

Funk Carioca (aka Baile funk)

What's not to love about hypnotically simple, early-
hip-hop/late-funk beats, and remarkably crude lyrics
about car stereos and big asses? Younger readers
more familiar with Crunk and Baltimore House might
find it too hokey and cheerful, but *funk carioca* is really
a revival of Miami Bass, where all that dirty south shit
got started.

Ibiza

Thanks to mammoth dance clubs like Manumission
(capacity 10,000) and various electronic-music
festivals, this resort island in Baleares, Spain has long
rivaled Berlin as the epicenter of Europe's dance club
culture. Its name, when used as an adjective, refers to
boiled-down, slightly sleazy house music somewhere
between vintage Detroit House and a car-commercial
version of Acid House.

THE GHETTOS)))

BARRIOS PERDIDOS

When you're searching for a good nightclub, you might want to avoid
straying into Latin American shantytowns, which tend to be druglord-
controlled autonomous zones way off the utility and police grids.

Grab your bulletproof vest and let's head to the **ghetto**.

Agarra tu chaleco antibalas y vámonos al/a la...

villa miseria [Arg]	*barrio* [DoR, Ven]
población callampa [Chi]	*tugurio* [Col, CoR]
barrio marginal [Ecu]	*barrio de chabolas* [Spn]
asentamiento [Gua]	*ciudad perdida, nopal, colonia popular* [Mex]
chacarita [Par]	*pueblo joven, asentamiento humano* [Per]
arrabal [PuR]	*cantegril* [Uru]

Salsa

Outside of a few specific places, *Salsa* is as dorky and pony-tailed as it is in suburban America, no matter how short the skirts, how high the heels, or how slutty the afterparties. I'm only including this among real pop genres to discourage some persistent rumors to the contrary.

•••••Computer-ese
Jerga informática

Like anywhere else in the world, most techie lingo is just barely transliterated English. But for the sake of teaching by example, here are the less obvious basic terms. If you really want to learn computer-ese, though, set the language to Spanish on your OS, your cell phone, and your software, and then teach yourself the hard way.

Does your apartment have **broadband**?
*¿Tu departamento tiene **banda ancha**?*
Cable predominates over DSL most everywhere, but both are usually called *banda ancha*.

There's a movie I've been trying to compress and **upload to you** on limewire.
*Hay una peli que vengo tratando de comprimir y **subirt** por limewire.*
Just as *subir* means "to upload," *bajar* means "to download."

My **home machine**'s totally fucked.
*Mi **compu de casa** está jodida.*

E-mail it to me as an **attachment** so I can **print it out**.
*Mándamelo como **archivo adjunto** para que lo pueda imprimir.*

Where'd you get that DVD that plays **bootlegs** and **DivX movies**?
*¿Donde conseguiste ese DVD que toca los **piratas** y los **divx**?*
Thanks to tiny SRT subtitle files that are legal to up- and download, international video piracy is now as easy as ripping the subtitle track off an American DVD. This allows Spanish-subtitled DivX files

to appear months before the official DVD releases, and makes it easy for Anime freaks to translate everything the studios don't.

Do I need a **password** to access your USB **pendrive**?
*¿Necesito **contraseña** para acceder tu **llavero** USB?*

My **off-brand player** holds twice as many MP3s as your **iPod**!
*¡Mi **reproductor de cuarta** guarda dos veces los MP3s que tu **iPod**!*

That **backdrop** is a little inappropriate, don't ya think?
*Ese **papel tapiz** es poco apropiado, ¿no te parece?*

Fifteen minutes of **Googling** and the damn **Wikipedia** doesn't qualify as "research."
*Quince minutos de **Googlear** y el pinche **Wiki** no cualifica como "investigación."*

The **link** you sent me took me to **tranny porn**!
*¡El **enlace** que me mandaste me llevó a **porno trave**!*

·····Text messaging
SMSeando

Text messaging is *huge* in Spanish-speaking lands—largely because neither Spaniards nor Latin Americans can afford to talk on the phone much, given the ruthless price-fixing and gouging of their telecom markets. Unfortunately for non-native speakers, spry youngsters keep raising the bar on cryptic abbreviations and acronyms.

I love you always	tq 100pre	*(te quiero siempre)*
What	q	*(que)*
Where	dde	*(donde)*
Here	ak	*(aquí)*
Because	xq	*(porque)*
I don't know	nc	*(no sé)*
No	—	*(no)*
Bye	xau	*(ciao)*
Hope you're well	ke tii bn/ktbn	*(que estés bien)*
Idiot	won	*(huevón)*

Shit	mela	[mierda]
I shit on you	tkg	[te cagué]
Suck it	xupalo	[chúpalo]
Your mother's pussy	ctm	[chocha	concha	coño de tu madre]

T kiero + q tdo l mndo, toy :D

Te quiero más que todo el mundo, estoy contento.
I love you more than all the world, I'm so happy.

M da =, won

Me da igual, huevón
It's the same to me, moron.

Uds fue a s bar nue? Dde qda?

¿Ustedes fueron a ese bar nuevo? ¿Dónde queda?
Did you guys go to that new bar? Where is it?

Qan2 m aqerde t qnto. Sta nfrmø tdv?

Cuando me acuerde te cuento. ¿Estás enfermo todavía?
I'll tell you when I remember. Are you still sick?

Stoi bn pro tmpko mxo mjor tqG

Estoy bien, pero tampoco mucho mejor. Te quiero, G.
I'm better, but not much better, either. Love, G.

POKƎMONƎSƎ)))

POKƐ-ƐMO

If you thought 'leet-speak was annoying (4nd wh0 d035nt?), wait till you see what horrible monstrosities have been unleashed on the Spanish language by Latin America's geeky obsession with Pokemon.

> **Kieeh beiioÓóoòòòh** *(¡qué bello!)*
> How pretty!
>
> **t0 R€sHhuLoNaÀhh** *(¡Está re-culona!)*
> She's got hella booty!
>
> **illoooooo ame un lerul!** *(¡'Elooo, dame un curo!)*
> Heeeey, gimme a buck!

·····Fashion
La moda

Although, or maybe because, half the world's sweatshops and *maquilladoras* are in Latin America, big-city Spanish-speakers can be as shallow and ruthless as any of those catty amateurs on *Project Runway*. Here are some basics for clawing and hissing.

The Twiggy look is totally **in vogue**—quit eating now!
*El estilo Twiggy está muy **en boga**—¡basta de comer, ya!*

Wearing a sports jersey to a funeral is pretty **tacky**.
*Ir a un entierro de camiseta deportiva es bien **chabacano**.*

Take off that beret, you look like a **yuppie** in midlife crisis!
*¡Quítate esa boina, pareces un **yuppie** en crisis de edad!*

Her **hipster** vibe is so fake. Her tattoos aren't even real!
*Su aire de **modernilla** es tan falso. ¡Falsos aun los tatuajes!* (Spn) | ...***cheta*** (S.Cone)

I pretend I'm not into all that **bling-bling**, but when I see platinum and ice like that....
*Disimulo cualquier interés en el **blinblineo**, pero cuando veo a platino y hielo así....*

Faux snakeskin is really **trendy** right now.
*Piel de serpiente falsa está bien **de moda** al momento.*

·····Youth cultures
Tribus urbanas

Los rockeros
Rock has a totally different meaning in every Hispanic culture. In Mexico, the boundaries between black metal, stoner-metal, punk, industrial, and butt-rock are pretty permeable, making anyone who likes any of the above a *rockero*. In Argentina, *rockeros* are specifically aficionados of *rock nacional*, as opposed to the imported stuff (mostly American) hogging the airwaves. So sporting a U2 shirt makes you a *rockero* in Mexico but a sell-out in Argentina.

Aggros

In Nu-Metal-crazed Chile, *los aggros* issued an ultimatum to *los rockeros*: Jettison your attachment to all rock subgenres that came before Nu Metal, throw out your Rolling Stones records, and stop washing your hair, or else we won't let you into our Worlds of Warcraft clan! Unfortunately, large numbers of the *huevones* took them up on it.

Los punkeros (aka ponkeros)

The robust tradition of anarchism in Spain trickled down to Latin America when Spanish anarchists fled there after the Spanish Civil War, turning anarchy into a real way of life rather than just a fashion statement, as it was in the U.K. Latin American punks are therefore a little more rebellious than their Anglo counterparts, less likely to get a job, and more likely to end up making pipe bombs than just silk-screening edgy slogans onto patches.

Los marquitos

Subcomandante Marcos, leader of the Zapatista movement, maintains semianonymity to this day. After those massive "we are all Marcos" rallies where flash-mobs would don the Zapatista ski-mask "uniform," would-be Marcoses became affectionately known as *Marquitos*. But this pet name is slowly becoming reserved for middle-class posers who sport Che Guevara shirts and mall-bought Mayan man-purses, and who use their English tutors to translate Rage Against the Machine lyrics.

Los "darks" (aka moribundos, góticos)

Goths are different in the Hispanic world, mostly because black lace is more grandma than edgy, and fake blood is a bit mundane after all the civil wars and the weekly "blood-drinking" at Mass. Hispanic goths are more into serial killers, sadomasochism, politics, and banned horror films than Victorian kitsch, burlesque, and séances. And they prefer to make their own clothes rather than shop at Hot Topic.

Los bakalas; los bakaleros
Once slang for "fresh," as in "fresh as Bilbao *bacalao* (cod)," this term then came to refer nostalgically to the golden age of Spanish dance club culture. Nowadays, though, Spaniards use the word to refer derogatorily to MDMA burnouts and tacky 16-year-olds bumpin' goa-trance in their lowered Hondas.

Los emos (aka *sensibles*)
Yup, same as at your high school—the sensitive kids wear sweaters and Converse All-Stars. They like sappy screamo and they slouch a lot. Their doting moms probably sewed those precious little homemade patches onto their Jansports for them. Recently, Mexican emos have borne the brunt of nationwide mob violence at the hands of *punkeros* and *rockeros* who are sick of them "biting their style." (No, really—emos are getting the shit kicked out of them in bloody riots over who pierced what first!)

Los niños bien, aka *el chetaje* (S.Cone), *los yeyés* (Pan), *los pijos* (Spn)
Yes, even the poorest corners of Spain and Latin America boast a robust leisure class, and each country has its own name for the bunch. This group tends more to the over-tanned-Eurotrash, stone-washed-jeans look than the American country-club preppy set.

Los poperos (aka *poppis*)
Want to stick out with a glossy subcultural persona without all the conflict of being anti-anything? Why not join the rank and file of the prettyboys and babydolls who can't think of anything better to identify with than asinine Shakira-style pop music! It's "hurrah for everything" every day for these perky little bottles of Prozac.

CHAPTER 8

SPORTY SPANISH
ESPAÑOL DEPORTISTA

·····Soccer
Fútbol

Wherever Spanish is spoken, there is only one sport—football. Not the kind with quarterbacks and piles of sweaty men gangbanging each other on the field nickel defenses, but the *real* kind: *fútbol*. Many of the key terms used to talk about football are easy enough for an English speaker to pick up because, well, they're English words, including that monosyllabic word that sports announcers belt out for 90 seconds at a time.

> **Who's your favorite...?**
> *¿Cuál es tu...favorito?*
>
> **I wanna kill that...!**
> *¡Quiero matar a ese...!*
>
> That...is **legit.**
> *Es **chévere** ese...* (Mex, Carib) | *...**bárbaro**...* (S.Cone, Andes)

That...sucks.
Es una mierda ese...

team
equipo

franchise
club

forward
delantero/a
This is the guy who scores all the goals, take his shirt off, and goes running around the field with his arms out like an airplane.

defender
defensa
This is one of the guys who plays in back and has thighs like tree trunks.

sweeper
líbero/a
This guy is the last line of defense between the defensive line and the goalie.

goalie
portero/a | golero/a (Mex)
If you don't know what a goalie is, you probably shouldn't even be reading this book.

coach
entrenador/a

referee
árbitro/a

How do I get to the **stadium/court**?
*¿Cómo llego a la **cancha**?*

Come on, let's see how cheap tickets are from that **scalper**.
*¡Vamonos!, a ver como están de baratas las entradas de ese **revendedor/a**.*

Wanna grab a beer **at halftime**?
*¿Quieres conseguir una cerveza **entre medios**?*

Number 9 scored **a hell of a goal**.
*El nueve metió **un golazo**.*

What's the **score**?
*¿Y el **tanteo**?*

Their team **scored** two goals.
*Su equipo **marcó** dos goles.*

Goooooooooaaaaaaaaalllllllllllllllllllllllllllllllllllllllllll!
¡Goooooooooooooooooooooolllllllllllllllllllllllllllllll!
The *goooooooooooooool*-yelling tradition, which seems so
timeless, was actually limited to Argentine radio and TV until the
1990 World Cup, when an Argentine (and Boca-loyal) sportscaster,
Andrés Cantor, set the standard by which all future sportscasters
would be measured. Like opera singing, it's all in the diaphragm
muscle.

·····For the fans
Para los hinchas

Who do you **root for**?
*¿A quién **apoyas**? | ¿Por quién **hinchas**?* (S.Cone)

I'm a fan of Boca.
***Soy hincha de** Boca.*
Hincha is a term used only for soccer fans. For all other sports,
fans are either *fanáticos* or *aficionados*.

You're one of those **hardcore, crazy fans**, aren't you?
*Tú eres uno des esos "**ultras**," ¿no?*
Ultra as in *ultrafanático*, the chest-painting kind.

I'm not a **hooligan** or anything like that. (the violent,
rioting kind)
*No, **gamberro** no soy, ni nada al estilo.*

KNOCK-DOWN, DRAG-OUT RiVALRi2S)))

RIVALIDADES A BRAZO PARTIDO

You can't have a team without a rival team. And you can't have a rivalry without a major, annual showdown that divides the country in half.

Mexican League: Guadalajara vs. Club América

Guadalajarans think of Mexico City as a city full of wannabe Europeans. Residents of Mexico City consider Guadalajara to be the backward epicenter of country music, working-class culture, and all things rural and "old school." Guada's team, *las chivas*, almost never drafts a player born outside of México. Club América's team, *las aguilas*, has a roster full of ringers poached from the international circuit and European leagues. The match between these two teams restages the major political struggle of Mexican history, as evidenced in their nicknames: *los capitalinos y los provincianos*, or, the Capital City kids and the Backswoodsmen.

Argentine League: Boca vs. River

These two Buenos Aires teams have been the major Argentine clubs for over a century. Boca, the name taken from the warehouse neighborhood at the mouth (*boca*) of the River Plata, are working-class heroes who've adopted the nickname *bosteros*, "manure-shovelers." River, based among the English-speaking, country-club elites on the North (i.e., river) side of the city, is nicknamed *los millionarios*. The annual *"superclásico"* is such a spectator event that travel agencies sell package deals structured around it. But bring your riot gear! The mythology surrounding the teams sometimes turns the postgame riot into all-out class warfare. Whichever teams loses gets mercilessly ridiculed on banners hung out of windows in the following weeks.

Spanish League: Barcelona vs. Real Madrid

The two biggest, most successful teams in Spain face off twice a year, pitting the two major cities of Spain and the two poles of Spanish life: Castilian civility vs. Cataluñian anarchy, standard Spanish vs. Catalán, and mainstream politics vs. separatist solidarity. Team Barcelona, nicknamed Barça, is called the *culers* or *culés*, because their popularity outgrew their tiny stadium in the '20s when anyone walking by saw the *culos* of the last fans to arrive hanging over the stadium wall. Team Madrid, made up of pretty-boys in white uniforms, gets called *los merengues* and sports a prominent royal crown on its team crest— which might handicap its popularity if only they weren't so amazingly good (they hold the record for most European Cup titles). Whenever these two teams face off, Spanish life comes screeching to a halt to see who will win.

That fuckin' **ref** doesn't see anything!
*¡Ese **silbante** de mierda cagó no ve nada!*
Literally, "whistleblower"

I can barely hear you, everyone's **cheering so loud**!
*¡Apenas te oigo, todos están **alentando tan fuerte**!*

Look at the other team's **supporters**! They're gonna cry any minute!
*¡Mira **la barra** del otro club! ¡Se van echar a llorar!*

We are **the champions**!
*¡Somos **los/las campeones/as**!*

·····"He's on fire!"
"¡Está que le sale!"

Half the fun of sports is the whole panoply of specialized cursing and poetic imagery that goes with it. Here are some basics to help get you started on the long road to decoding the banter of play-by-play announcers and Sportscenter repeats. And just for the record, anybody who says *enfuego* to describe a player on a hot streak would be laughed at like they just crapped the bed.

They're really **showing some hustle**!
*¡Se están **poniendo las pilas**!*
Literally, "putting in their batteries"

He's on a helluva **streak**!
*¡Está en una buena **racha**!*

Get your fat ass in gear!
¡Muévete las nalgas anchas!

Get aross the field, already!
*¡Dale, **corta campo**!*

That referee is **blind as a bat**!
*¡Ese árbitro es un **murciélago**!*

Their defense is **pudding**.
*Su defensa es **un flan**.*

That defender's a real **pushover**.
*Ese defensa es un **queso** total.*

That forward **is stiff as a cast**.
*Ese delantero **es de yeso**.*

Check out **leadfoot** over there.
*Mira al **patadura** ese.*

He's total **deadweight**.
*El es un **muerto** total.*

What an **oaf**!
*¡Qué **zafio/a**! | ...**croto** (S.Cone)*

Stop being such a **crybaby**!
*¡Basta de hacerte el/la **llorón/as**!*

You call that offense, you **pussyfooting dandy**?
*¿Así juegas ofensa, **pechofrío remilgado**?*

They totally **demolished** us.
*Nos **dieron masa**.*
This actually means "they fucked us" — sports are as homoerotic
in Spanish as in any language.

Did you see that **lob**? How the hell did he make **the
nationals**?
*¿Viste a esa **masita**? ¿Cómo carajo llegó **a la [liga]
nacional**?*

They're really **putting up a fight**!
*¡Mira si están **dándoles lucha**!*

It's gonna be **a fight to the bloody end**, fellas!
*¡Será **una lucha sin cuartel**, muchachos!*

·····Second-rate sports
Deportes de segunda

In most Spanish-speaking lands, anything but *fútbol* isn't
really on the level of a "major sport." And if Spain weren't
part of Europe, tennis and fencing and all those other fancy
boy sports wouldn't even be tolerated. So if you go asking
around for a baseball diamond and get only blank stares,
it's not because you're using the wrong word — it's because
you're in the wrong place.

I play…
Yo juega al/a la…

I do…
Yo hago el/la…

Wanna go play some…?
¿Quieres ir a jugar…?

Is there any…on TV?
¿Hay…en la tele?

boxing
el boxeo

racquetball
el squash
Technically, squash isn't racquetball, but people will be more likely to know what you're talking about if you ask them where you can play "squash."

basketball
el baloncesto

tennis
el tenis

fencing
la esgrima

baseball
el béisbol

swimming
la natación

karate
el karate

pro wrestling
la lucha libre

ultimate fighting
la lucha hardcore

Careful, I'm a **black belt**.
*Cuídate, que soy **cinturón negro**.*

I can **break boards** with my head.
*Puedo **romper tablas** con la cabeza.*

Cheerleading is too a sport!
¡Sí, que porrismo es un deporte!

He blasted that **home run**.
Lanzó ese jonrón.

It's going, going, gone! That's a **roundtripper**!
¡Se va, se va, y se fué! ¡Es un cuadrangular!

Did you see that **slam dunk**?
¿Viste a ese clavado?

·····Other sports
Otros deportes

Uruguayans kick ass at...
Los uruguayos son fenomenales en...

Colombians can't play...for shit.
Los colombianos jugando...son una mierda.

Polo
Polo still looms big at the country-club end of the sports spectrum in Latin America. Since the Latin- and Anglo-American championships merged in 1987, Argentina and Brazil have won all but one title, with Chile and Mexico helping to keep America, England, and Australia out of the top three (except for one blip in 1995). According to urban myth, polo aficionado Sylvester Stallone owns over one quarter of the grassy Argentine province of Rio Negro, where he makes a killing raising world-class polo horses.

Kayak-polo
Yes, it's what you're thinking, and Spain has two televised competitive leagues of it.

Cesta-punta
This Basque variant of *jai alai* holds the Guinness world record for manually propelled ball speed: In 1979 someone threw a *pelota* out of a cyborg-looking

basket-mitt at 188 mph! Rubber balls flung at that speed will break any bone they hit if you get between the thrower and the wall.

Pok-ta-pok
This Olmecan sport makes rugby look like a tea party. Each team has to somehow get a heavy, hemorrhage-inducing leather ball across an H-shaped court and through a hoop it barely fits in without using their hands or feet (tip: it's all in the elbows). The sport is played by Mayan-speaking communities throughout Southern Mexico and Guatemala. A few teams toured Germany in 2006, trying to stir up international interest in the sport. Maybe they need to bring back the human-sacrifice component to get over the low-scoring doldrums.

Lacrosse
Argentina and Spain both hold national championships and send teams to the world championships. Although they may not be able to hold their own against the American, Canadian, and Iroquois teams when they get there, they are heroes back home for even qualifying.

Rugby
Another tooth-loosener that Argies and Spaniards really get behind is rugby, that sport with all the man-hugging, dog-piling, and fabulous stripey shirts. If it didn't involve so much facial scarring, it could almost be considered fruity.

Béisbol
It's no coincidence that some of the best Major League Baseball players come from the Caribbean. Baseball is huge in Puerto Rico, the Dominican Republic, and Cuba. Outside the Caribbean, though, don't expect to find anyone who wants to trade cards with you.

Lucha Libre
México's *luchas libres* are just as fake and theatrical as any WWF event, but the Mexican theatrical flair really comes out in the populist speeches the fighters deliver...*and* the vicious grandmothers in the audience screaming for blood.

•••••Working out
Haciendo ejercicios

Not into the whole team-sports thing? Prefer sweating in a room full of mirrors with tacky '80s music blaring and perverts pretending not to stare at you? Lucky for you, gym culture has caught on everywhere. Nowadays, you can even find gyms in places that barely have running water.

Where is/are...?
¿Dónde queda/quedan...?

the treadmill
las trotadoras | la caminadoras (Mex) | *la cintas de correr* (Spn)

the stair machine
la escaladora

the exercise bike
la bicicleta estacionaria

the freeweights
los pesas libres

OTHER ACTIVITIES)))

I'M WAY INTO...
SOY MUY METIDO EN LO DE...

yoga	*el yoga*
backpacking	*el "trekking"*
hiking	*el senderismo*
road biking	*el bicicletismo*
jogging	*el "footing"*
darts	*los dardos*
foosball/table football	*el futbolín/el metegol*
pool	*el billar*
ping pong	*el ping pong*

the bench press
la banca

the pool
la piscina | *la pileta* (S.Cone) | *la alberca* (Mex)

I just did 1000...
Acabo de hacer mil...

push-ups
las flexiones | *las lagartijas* (Mex)
"*Lagartijas*" literally means "lizards," which makes sense, since lizards are always kinda bobbing up and down on their arms

pull-ups
las dominadas

sit-ups
los abdominales ; las sentadillas

You're looking **ripped**!
*¡Te ves **macizo/a**!*

He must **work out**.
*Debe **entrenarse**.*

First, I'm gonna **stretch**.
*Primero, voy a **desperezarme**.*

Wanna **go for a jog**?
*¿Quieres **salir a correr**?* | *¿Quieres **salir a trotar**?* (Mex)

I'm **out of breath, sore, and need a cigarette** desperately.
*Estoy **sin aliento, dolorido, y necesito un cigarrillo** desesperadamente.*

CHAPTER 9

HUNGRY SPANISH
CASTELLANO HAMBRIENTO

Spanish-speakers aren't pretentious or finicky about their food. They like honest fare cooked home-style, just the way Mamá made it. And they really like to see their food being made—pre-cooked food is considered an abomination in most places.

•••••Hunger
Hambre

I'm starving.
Estoy hambriento/a.

I'm dying of hunger/thirst.
Me estoy muriendo *de hambre/sed.*

Let's get some...
Vamos a conseguirnos algo de...

> **food**
> *comida*

> **grub / eats**
> *manduca*

junk food
comida basura | comida chatarra (LatAm)

fast food
comida rápida | minutas (S.Cone)

street food
garnacha (Mex)

ethnic food
comida étnica

I'm full.
Estoy lleno/a.

I'm stuffed.
Estoy repleto/a.

I'm gonna burst!
¡Estoy quebrado/a!

Yum-yum!
¡Ñam-ñam!

It's really good!
¡Está buenísimo!

That was…
Eso era…

a good meal
una buena comida

really tasty
muy sabroso

delicious
delicioso

scrumptious
riquísimo

filling
saciante

Yuck!
¡Qué asco!

Their food is crap.
Su comida es una mierda.

It's disgusting.
Es un asquete.

A farmhand **wouldn't eat that shit** in the middle of a drought!
*¡Un peón **no comería esa mierda** en plena sequía!*

I'm not gonna eat...
No voy a comer...

> **this bullshit**
> *esta bosta*
> Literally, "manure"

> **this revolting garbage**
> *esta basura inmunda*

> **that abomination**
> *esa abominación*

> **this steaming turd**
> *esta cagada humeante*

•••••At the restaurant
En el restaurante

Service in the Spanish-speaking world isn't *bad*—it just doesn't give a shit about you. That's because there's no incentive, since tips in most of Latin America range from whatever coins come back in your change to a whopping 10 percent. It's not even that rude to leave no tip if you're short that week. But tip or no tip, the waitstaff won't "wait" on you: They do their own thing until you call, and if they don't like how you call them over, they play deaf, look busy, or pick up the phone to call their girlfriend.

Bring me...
Tráeme...

> **the menu** (more formal)
> *la carta*
>
> **the menu** (less formal)
> *el menú*
> In much of South America, the lunch or dinner special is also called *el menu*.

THERE'S A WORM IN MY TEQUILA. CALL...)))

HAY UN GUSANO EN MI TEQUILA. LLÁMAME...

the manager	*el gerente*
your boss	*tu jefe*
the chef	*el chef*

If they actually pronounce it in proper French, you're probably paying too much for your food.

the cook	*el cocinero*
the waiter /waitress	*el camarero/a*
the dimwit that took my order	*el/la lelo/a que me tomó el orden*
the wine steward	*el/la sommelier*

It's French, and he probably is, too; you're not at a place serving local specialties.

| the barbecue master | *el/la asador/a* |

This is a proud profession and a guarded position in most of Latin America. The BBQ master ranks even higher than the chef in most kitchens.

the check
la cuenta

a bread basket
una canasta de pan

some steamed tortillas
algunas tortillas al vapor

the silverware
los cubiertos

Can we **order**?
*¿Podemos **pedir**?*

What would you recommend to a first-timer?
*¿**Qué recomendarías** a un principiante?*

Tell me, does "*cuy*" mean **guinea pig**?
*Dime, ¿ "cuy" quiere decir **conejo de la India**?*

Five bucks if you can **name every organ** in my bowl of menudo.
*Cincuenta pesos si me puedes **nombrar cada órgano** en mi plato de menudo.*

What's taking so long? **Did they head out to the farm** to find my chicken, or what?
*¿Qué demora tanto? ¿**Se fueron al rancho** para elegir la gallina, o qué?*

THE NOT-SO-UNIVERSAL LANGUAGE OF GRUB)))

GRUB	TO GRUB/CHOW DOWN
El refín (Mex)	*Refinar | echar papa* (Mex)
El pipirín | el merol (CenAm)	*Jamar* (CenAm)
El papeo | la jala (Spn)	*Jalar; jamar | papear* (Spn)
La manya (S.Cone)	*Morfar | manyar* (S.Cone)
La jama (Andes)	*Jamear; combear | papear* (Andes)
La jama | el pasto (Carib)	*Jamar* (Carib)

I don't have any dough on me, but I could **do the dishes** to settle up.

*No tengo nada de billullo conmigo, pero podría **lavar los platos** para ajustar la cuenta.*

·····Mystery meats
Carnes ocultas

Much to the chagrin of Texas, "barbecue" isn't even an English word. *Barbacoa* was an old Latin American custom brought across the Rio Grande by Mexican cowherds, who, along with their counterparts in Spain and South America, had been getting their grill on for centuries. And after all that time heating their meat, they've come up with some pretty, um, "interesting" things to grill. We raise our forks to you, daring *asadores*!

Grill me up some…
Tírame un poco de… en la parrilla.

How much protein is there in…?
¿Cuánta proteina hay en el…?

I'm on a strict diet of…
Estoy a dieta estricta de…

> **Chicharrón:** Deep-fried strips of pork skin or thicker cuts

> **Molleja:** Sweetbreads (i.e., the thymus gland of a young lamb or calf). It's pretty safe to eat these in Latin America (especially in Argentina and Uruguay) where ranchers often exceed organic standards.

> **Butifarra:** A peppery pork sausage. The white variety is made entirely of lean pork, while the black kind is packed with pork fat and blood.

> **Morcilla:** Coagulated blood sausage. Consider yourself warned.

> **Garrobo:** A kind of iguana, usually served in a broth.

> **Callos:** A Spanish form of tripe (i.e., beef stomach) from a younger, less world-weary digestive tract. Mmmm!

Chinchulines:
Chunks of barbecued intestine. You may wanna check that they've been completely emptied.

Cuy: Guinea pig. In rural parts of the Andes, you'll find street vendors selling whole roasted guinea pigs out of their carts like hot dogs.

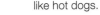

·····Street food
Comida callejera

Spanish speakers don't go in for fast food the way Americans do. Why deal with fluorescent lights, ugly uniforms, and zit-faced teens when you can buy cheaper food from a grizzled, one-eyed mountain man pushing a griddle around in a shopping cart? The food just tastes better that way.

I'm dying for a good...
Estoy muriendo por un buen...

Taco (México)
Think you know something about tacos just cuz you can say *carne asada*? You don't know shit. Not until you've tried tacos *al pastor* (spicy, spit-roasted pork), *tacos árabes* (in pita bread), tacos stuffed with spicy *papas* (bright-red mashed potatoes), *nopales* (cactus), *buche* (tripe), *ubre* (udder), *cuerno* (horn-skinflap), *bofe* (lung), *suadero* (skin left on!), *trompa* (lips), and *sesos* (brains). Makes your local *taquería* seem a little less authentic, no?

Huarache (Southern Mexico)
This Aztec forerunner of the modern taco is made thick from fresh yellow or blue corn, shaped like the sole of a sandal (hence the name), stuffed with a layer of black

beans, and topped with cheese, *salsa verde*, sautéed mushrooms, and squash flowers.

Pupusa (Honduras, Guatemala, El Salvador)

This handmade griddle-cake is like a *huarache* but bigger and perfectly round, often filled with *queso y loroco* (the sweet bud of a native vine), *queso y chipilín* (a savory herb), and *revueltas* (a combination of cheese, *chicharrón*, and sometimes refried beans). A good *pupusa* will fill you up like nobody's business.

Elote (Central America)

The name *elote* refers specifically to sweet-corn. When an *elotero* yells the word on the street, though, they're talkin' 'bout corn on the cob, boiled, roasted, or barbecued on a jerry-rigged shopping cart. Spice it up with room-temperature mayo, *cotija* cheese, *chilitos*, lime juice, salt, and *Tequesquite* (a pre-Columbian mineral salt).

Tamal (Central America, Andes)

The further south you go, the weirder tamales get. Banana leaf-steamed *tamales yucatecas* are stuffed with pork marrow, annatto seed, and sour orange stew. *Tamales pishques* have refried beans and ash stirred in with the cornmeal masa. The huge, intense Nicaraguan *nacatamal* has annatto-seed pork, rice, potatoes, mint, olives, and raisins. Some Andean tamales include peanuts, turtle meat, and African herbs, while in Northern Argentina the *masa* is half corn and half squash.

Atol (Central America)

The name *atol* refers to both chowdery soups and hot drinks, often sold out of giant soup thermoses pushed around in a baby stroller. The most common Mexican *atol* is *achampurrado*, a thick, modern form of Aztec hot cocoa (cinnamon, chile pepper, whole milk). In many countries you'll get a bowl of savory, bean-watery *atoles* when you buy *pupusas*, whether from a restaurant, a window counter, or some guy with an eye-patch pushing a shopping cart down the street.

Aguafresca (Central America)

These cooling, sugary beverages come in an infinite array of flavors, including hibiscus blossom, mango,

HOW WOULD YOU LIKE YOUR GUINEA PIG COOKED, SIR?)))

¿CÓMO LE COCINO EL CUY, SEÑOR?

Very rare	*Casi crudo ; sangriento* [bloody]
Rare	*Vuelta y vuelta* [barely flipped twice]
Medium-rare	*Un cuarto*
Medium	*A mitad ; a punto*
Medium-well	*Tres cuartos ; más cocido*
Well-done	*Bien cocido*
Burnt to a crisp	*Quemadito ; carbonizado*
Um, I'm a vegetarian.	*Eeeh, soy vegetariano.*

watermelon, tamarind, sugarcane, and papaya. You can even still find some of the pre-Columbian *aguasfrescas* like *tepache* (fermented pineapple rind and crude cane), *pinole* (sweet spices and roasted cornmeal), *lechuguilla* (a kind of agave cactus), and *tesgüino* (a malty corn-beer). Go for it, young adventurer!

Migas, aka ***migas de pastor*** (Southern Spain)
This couscous-like dish was traditionally made from hard bread and was cooked in a big pan with bacon or pigskin and a bunch of other meats, veggies, and even sweets like melon, grapes, or chocolate. It's not much to look at when the vendor is stirring it around with a big wooden stick, but trust me, it's legit.

Ceviche (Perú, Ecuador, México)
Perú is proud of its only major culinary export—few people outside Japan get this excited about raw fish. Ceviche is "cooked" by adding acidic vinegar and lime juice that kill more microbes than most "real" cooking. There are tons of regional variations, like the shellfish-and sea-snail-heavy Ecuadorian kind, or the uncannily black *conchas negras* ceviche served in a shell with *plátanos* or *batata* and toasted corn.

Paella (Spain)
This famous rice dish is named after the pan it's cooked in, a huge, shallow vat that evaporates out moisture quickly. The most famous paella, the saffron-laden Valencian kind, takes all day to cook and incorporates as many sea-snails and shellfish as the season allows. *Paella mixta* "mixes in" rabbit and chicken with the shellfish. And *arroz negro* is a *paella* dyed black with squid or cuttlefish ink, great for adventurous eaters and cephalopod buffs alike.

Bacalao al pil-pil (Northeastern Spain)
This freaky Basque dish involves slow-cooking big chunks of cod, garlic, and tiny chili peppers in tons of olive oil until the oil congeals into a gelatinous sauce. Basque doesn't have a word for the texture, which is probably why they made up the onomatopoetic "pil-pil." Or maybe someone just tried to trick their kids into eating it by giving it a cute name, 'cuz it's pretty damn gross.

Plátanos, aka *tajadas* (Caribbean, Central America)
Fried plaintains cut in strips (*tajadas*) to maximize the frying area *and* your cholesterol. Beware of *patacón pisao*: nasty, deep-fried, green plantain peel. *Tostones*, on the other hand, are delicious since they're mashed halfway through cooking to get a nice, varied texture.

•••••Other grub
Otras manducas

Let's face it, Spanish speakers are Catholics, and Catholics have a lot of mouths to feed. And there's no more efficient way to use all the scraps in the fridge than to throw together a sandwich, make a stew, or stuff last night's leftovers into some dough and bake it in the oven.

Go make me a...sandwich.
Anda a hacerme un sandwich...

Cubano (Caribbean)
The porkiest sandwich on earth! To make an old-school *cubano*, you take a roll shortened with pig-lard,

warm it in pig-lard on a griddle, and add swiss cheese, ham, and roast pork.

De miga (Argentina, Uruguay)
A crustless sandwich made from paper-thin slices of white bread, heavy on the mayo. The traditional fillings are ham, processed cheese, slices of oily pepper and/or palm hearts, lettuce, tomato, and an olivey egg salad. Throw one into a panini grill and you have the best snack every invented, known simply as *un tostado*.

De jamón serrano, aka **jamón curado** (Spain)
The ham in these sandwiches is dried and salt-cured for one to two years in whole hocks that often hang over the counter in a bar or deli. The prized *ibérico* variety is cured longer and made from pigs raised on a diet of grass and acorns (*bellotas*). Pair this with some dry cheese and you're in business.

Pambazo (Guadalajara)
This gut-busting local variation on the Mexican *torta* (a lighter "Cuban" with avocado, raw onion, and beans) ups the heartburn ante with peppery *chorizo*, hot sauce, and bright-red mashed potatoes.

YOU SAY TOMATO, I SAY JÍTOMATE)))

Throughout Latin America, particularly where each indigenous language is native, many fruits and veggies are still called by their pre-Columbian names instead of their standard Spanish ones.

Tomato (the big, firm kind)	*Jítomate* (Nahuatl)
Peanut	*Maní* (Taino)
Chili pepper	*Ají* (Taino)
Squash	*Ayote* (Nahuatl), *Pipián* (Mayan), *Zapallo* (Quechua)
Sweet potato	*Camote* (Nahuatl), *Boniato* (Taino)
Corn	*Elote* (Nahuatl), *Choclo* (Quechua)
Avocado	*Aguacate* (Nahuatl), *Palta* (Quechua)

Let's stew up some...
Pongámonos a guisar un/una...

Locro (Argentina, Bolivia, Paraguay)
A thick-as-peanut-butter stew featuring hominy,
beans, and often tendony shredded meat scraps.
When done right, it's amazing.

Ropa vieja (Cuba)
Fancy shredded pork stewed in a tomato-based
criollo sauce, with the texture of the tattered rags
your mom makes you throw out, hence the name
"Old Clothes."

Menudo (México)
Most of the organs in this stew (including the free-
floating eyeballs in some recipes) retain their shape
and appear whole in your bowl.

Mondongo (Venezuela, Colombia, Argentina, Uruguay)
Haggis with yucca, cornmeal cakes, and exotic purple
potatoes.

Posole aka **pozol** (Southern México, Honduras,
Guatemala)
A pork stew with hominy and pig organs slow-cooked
in a chili-chicken broth. At the last minute, you dump in
tons of fresh oregano, lime juice, and onion. The guest
of honor gets a big piece of pig's face in their bowl,
and everyone else who gets a foot gets good luck (or
something).

Chupe (Bolivia, Perú, Colombia, Paraguay, Chile,
Panamá)
This is a general term for various buttery, white soups,
made with barley, corn, or other grains, plus enough
big chunks of meat that you'll need a knife to go along
with your spork.

Olla podrida (Western Spain)
The name of the dish literally means, "putrid pot"
(and boy, am I hungry now!). It's a rich red-bean stew
thickened with bacon, blood sausage, and smoked
pig's ear, rib, and snout. Nothing says delicious like
pig snout.

Your moms sure knows how to bake a mean...
Sí que tu vieja sabe hornear una buena...

Sope, aka *pellizcada, picadita* (México)
This is like a taco-pizza—almost twice as large as a taco, thicker (and still soft and gooey inside), turned up at the edges like a pizza crust, and topped evenly instead of mounded like a taco.

Gordita (México)
Imagine a hot-pocket made by flash-frying a stuffed hand-made tortilla, then cutting it in half and stuffing in cheese while it's still hot enough to melt it, then baking it to a crisp.

Empanada (Southern Cone, Colombia)
The Argentine variety is best described as a hand-held calzone. They're usually filled with ham and cheese, spiced meat, spinach, or *humita* (a sweet-corn white sauce). Chilean ones are more like flakey meat turnovers, and Colombian ones are like English potpies, usually fried instead of baked. Central Americans use the term for any number of baked things, from oven-quesadillas to pies to casseroles.

·····Other Ulysses Press Titles

Dirty Chinese: Everyday Slang from "What's Up?" to "F*%# Off!"
MATT COLEMAN & EDMUND BACKHOUSE, **$10.00**

Dirty Chinese features phrases for every situation, even expressions to convince a local official that you have waited long enough and tipped him plenty already. A pronunciation guide, a reference dictionary and sample dialogues make this guide invaluable for those traveling to China.

Dirty French: Everyday Slang from "What's Up?" to "F*%# Off!"
ADRIEN CLAUTRIER AND HENRY ROWE, **$10.00**

With enough insults and swear words to offend every person in France without even speaking to them in English (which they really dislike), *Dirty French* has phrases for every situation, including expressions for describing art that make one sound smart and cool.

Dirty German: Everyday Slang from "What's Up?" to "F*%# Off!"
DANIEL CHAFFEY, **$10.00**

Dirty German provides enough insults to offend every person in Germany—without even mentioning that the Japanese make better cars—as well as explicit sex terms that'll even embarrass the women of Hamburg's infamous red light district.

Dirty Italian: Everyday Slang from "What's Up?" to "F*%# Off!"
GABRIELLE EUVINO, $10.00

Nobody speaks in strictly formal address anymore. Certainly not in Italy, where the common expression shouted on the streets is far from textbook Italian. This book fills in the gap between how people really talk in Italy and what Italian language students are taught.

Dirty Japanese: Everyday Slang from "What's Up?" to "F*%# Off!"
MATT FARGO, $10.00

Even in traditionally minded Japan, slang from its edgy pop culture constantly enter into common usage. This book fills in the gap between how people really talk in Japan and what Japanese language students are taught.

Dirty Russian: Everyday Slang from "What's Up?" to "F*%# Off!"
ERIN COYNE & IGOR FISUN, $10.00

Nothing is censored in *Dirty Russian*. This invaluable guide for off-the-beaten-path travelers going to Russia is packed with enough insults and swear words to offend every person in Russia without even mentioning that they lost the Cold War.

To order these books call 800-377-2542 or 510-601-8301, fax 510-601-8307, e-mail ulysses@ulyssespress.com, or write to Ulysses Press, P.O. Box 3440, Berkeley, CA 94703. All retail orders are shipped free of charge. California residents must include sales tax. Allow two to three weeks for delivery.

·····About the Authors

Juan Caballero is a doctoral candidate in Comparative Literature whose studies have spanned the Argentine novel, psychoanalysis, sadomasochism, linguistics, film noir, third-world aesthetics, and socialist revisionism. He is a lifelong Californian and avid backpacker, whose passions include competitive eating, contemporary art, noise music, booty-shakin', and internet porn.

Nick Denton-Brown loves talking dirty…in Spanish, probably because he was a Latin American Studies major at a school whose mascot is the missionary. He lives in Oakland, CA and loves eating burritos, playing soccer, and rocking out to Bruce Springsteen, in that order.